"In this little gem of a book, beginners will learn dozens of creative directives for solving a host of familiar clinical problems; more experienced therapists will marvel at how subtly these directives address underlying structural issues."

—Michael P. Nichols, Professor of Psychology,
College of William & Mary

"Haley and Richeport-Haley's new book provides an excellent presentation on the current state of thought on directive therapy. It is a brief, witty, and wise account that is a must-read for clinicians, teachers, students, and mental health historians. The book is a mixed blessing as it not only presents Jay Haley's latest ideas, but also his last. It is a fitting conclusion to his body of work. As with his earlier works, it will keep therapists talking for years to come."

—Joseph L. Wetchler, PhD, Professor and Director,
Marriage and Family Therapy Program,
Purdue University, Calumet

"This charming volume, containing a brief orientation to many of the key issues involved in Haley's strategic approach, case after case arranged along a life-cycle continuum, plus fascinating interviews illuminating key figures and moments in the history of family therapy, should spark the imagination of readers interested in changing the interaction between people to bring about positive outcomes."

—Michael F. Hoyt, PhD, Author of *Some Stories Are Better Than Others* and *Interviews with Brief Therapy Experts*

"Of all the people involved in psychotherapy whom I have ever known, Jay Haley and Milton Erickson were the only ones who knew and could explain what they were doing in ways people could understand. In *Directive Family Therapy*, there are no hidden meanings or psychobabble, just clear communication and the truth—a light shining in the darkness!"

—John H. Frykman, PhD, Author of *A New Connection* and *The Hassle Handbook—A Guide Through the Teenage Years*

CW00683585

NOTES FOR PROFESSIONAL LIBRARIANS AND LIBRARY USERS

This is an original book title published by The Haworth Press, Inc. Unless otherwise noted in specific chapters with attribution, materials in this book have not been previously published elsewhere in any format or language.

CONSERVATION AND PRESERVATION NOTES

All books published by The Haworth Press, Inc., and its imprints are printed on certified pH neutral, acid-free book grade paper. This paper meets the minimum requirements of American National Standard for Information Sciences-Permanence of Paper for Printed Material, ANSI Z39.48-1984.

DIGITAL OBJECT IDENTIFIER (DOI) LINKING

The Haworth Press is participating in reference linking for elements of our original books. (For more information on reference linking initiatives, please consult the CrossRef Web site at www.crossref.org.) When citing an element of this book such as a chapter, include the element's Digital Object Identifier (DOI) as the last item of the reference. A Digital Object Identifier is a persistent, authoritative, and unique identifier that a publisher assigns to each element of a book. Because of its persistence, DOIs will enable The Haworth Press and other publishers to link to the element referenced, and the link will not break over time. This will be a great resource in scholarly research.

Directive Family Therapy

Haworth Series in Brief & Solution-Focused Therapies
Yvonne M. Dolan, MA
Editor

Directive Family Therapy

Jay Haley
Madeleine Richeport-Haley

The Haworth Press, Inc.
New York

For more information on this book or to order, visit
http://www.haworthpress.com/store/product.asp?sku=5883

or call 1-800-HAWORTH (800-429-6784) in the United States and Canada
or (607) 722-5857 outside the United States and Canada

or contact orders@HaworthPress.com

Reprint 2007
The Haworth Press, Inc., 10 Alice Street, Binghamton, NY 13904-1580.

PUBLISHER'S NOTE
The development, preparation, and publication of this work has been undertaken with great care. However, the Publisher, employees, editors, and agents of The Haworth Press are not responsible for any errors contained herein or for consequences that may ensue from use of materials or information contained in this work. The Haworth Press is committed to the dissemination of ideas and information according to the highest standards of intellectual freedom and the free exchange of ideas. Statements made and opinions expressed in this publication do not necessarily reflect the views of the Publisher, Directors, management, or staff of The Haworth Press, Inc., or an endorsement by them.

Identities and circumstances of individuals discussed in this book have been changed to protect confidentiality.

Cover design by Kerry E. Mack.

Library of Congress Cataloging-in-Publication Data

Haley, Jay.
    Directive family therapy / Jay Haley, Madeleine Richeport-Haley.
        p. ; cm.
    Includes bibliographical references.
    ISBN: 978-0-7890-3355-0 (hard : alk. paper)
    ISBN: 978-0-7890-3356-7 (soft : alk. paper)
    1. Family psychotherapy. I. Richeport-Haley, Madeleine. II. Title.
    [DNLM: 1. Family Therapy—methods. WM 430.5F2 H168d 2007]

    RC488.5.H314 2007
    616.89'156—dc22

                                                              2007010700

To
Kristina Erickson, MD

ABOUT THE AUTHORS

Jay Haley, PhD, was a professor at the California School of Professional Psychology, Alliant International University. He was a professor at Stanford University, Howard University, and the University of Maryland. He was widely acclaimed as a pioneering therapist, master teacher, the chief architect of strategic therapy, and one of the founders of family therapy. He was the author of 21 books, more than 100 papers translated into 15 languages, and many films. He was director of training at the Philadelphia Child Guidance Clinic, co-founder of the Family Therapy Institute in Washington, DC, and founder of *Family Process,* the basic journal in the field. Dr. Jay Haley passed away in 2007.

Madeleine Richeport-Haley, PhD, is an anthropologist filmmaker who trained with Milton Erickson. She collaborated with her husband, Jay Haley, for 18 years, producing therapy training films and the book *The Art of Strategic Therapy.* She has been an invited faculty member of the Milton H. Erickson Foundation conferences and on the faculty of San Diego State University; the Federal University of Brazil, Natal; and University of Miami, Department of Psychiatry. Her work includes serving as a mental health consultant to WHO, *National Geographic,* and documentaries appearing on PBS. Her numerous publications have added a cross-cultural healing perspective to the therapy field.

CONTENTS

Foreword

Directive Family Therapy is an extraordinary manual for any experienced or beginning clinician who wants to master this innovative orientation. The introduction offers a concise presentation of the major ideas and issues that have occupied the field of therapy during the past forty years. This account of the notions that guide therapy and their mutations provides a foundation for the cases discussed in the rest of the book.

The cases are examined within the family life-cycle framework well known to Haley's readers. The emphasis is on shaping responsible directives that are used not only to stimulate change, but to set its direction and adjust its trajectory.

To read this book is to discover new problem-solving possibilities for our own cases, and to see that a quick and efficient grasp of knowledge from different sectors of a client's social situation is necessary in order to fashion productive directives. The therapist employs a flexible "broadband" mind.

Add the cases presented here to those in Haley's previous books and you will have a comprehensive casebook series on the repairs of assorted problems of the human condition at all levels of development. The couples cases, in particular, shine as a tour de force of the best of problem-solving imagination. The segments from past interviews with Haley, in Appendix A, are priceless. In them, he explains where, how, and with whom he created his ideas.

Braulio Montalvo, MA

Directive Family Therapy
Published by The Haworth Press, Inc., 2007. All rights reserved.
doi:10.1300/5883_a

Acknowledgments

Jay Haley died peacefully in his sleep on February 13, 2007. He was eighty-three years old. We had finished this book before he died and he was looking forward to its publication. When asked what he wanted his legacy to be, he responded, "to be the oldest living teacher of therapy." Although not the oldest, he did enjoy teaching into his eighties at the California School of Professional Psychology, Alliant International University. Our appreciation to the University and to the administrative wisdom of Scott Woolley.

Jay recorded his conversations with Dr. Milton H. Erickson over seventeen years. I also studied with Erickson and benefited from his feedback on my anthropological fieldwork. The therapeutic mastery of Erickson is present throughout this book. After his death in 1980, the friendship of his wife Elizabeth Erickson and the Erickson family continued, and has been invaluable to both of us.

The ideas presented here have been generated over fifty years of therapy and in many ways represent a revolution in the therapy field because they represent a willingness to think in new ways. In the 1950s, when Jay always said "everything happened," Gregory Bateson's Research Project began and together with John Weakland, Don Jackson doing therapy with psychotics, and the Zen ideas of Alan Watts, a communicative view of therapy was established. In the mid-1960s, Jay Haley moved to the Philadelphia Child Guidance Clinic for ten years and collaborated with Salvador Minuchin and Braulio Montalvo in training therapists and paraprofessionals. We want to thank Braulio Montalvo for his friendship and critique of this book.

Directive Family Therapy
Published by The Haworth Press, Inc., 2007. All rights reserved.
doi:10.1300/5883_b

We acknowledge the cooperation of students and colleagues who agreed to be supervised in this approach. Students like Neil Schiff became colleagues and friends and continued collaboration in seeing cases. Whether their names are mentioned or not, without this supervision learning process, these cases could not be written.

Special thanks to the editorial staff at The Haworth Press, to Patricia Brown for her conscientious attention to detail, and to Yvonne Dolan and Terry Trepper for their enthusiasm and consultation on this book.

Introduction

This is both an exciting and a perplexing time in therapy. There are countless schools of therapy to choose from, each with its own approach to helping clients. It is useful to consider the similarities and differences in the various schools of therapy when choosing ways to solve problems, because therapy has changed in surprising ways over the years. This book presents a therapy plan based upon the client following certain directives to resolve a problem.

As I (J. H.) look back, I am amazed to see the ways in which directive and traditional approaches to therapy are opposite each other. One can note how curious this is by just listing these differences. Although quite a few of the ideas of directive family therapy are mainstream today, a number of therapists adhere to many of the premises that I am calling traditional.

* * *

Long-term therapy vs. brief therapy. Brief therapy was once considered to be shallow and failing at deep therapy; long-term therapy was the fashion. Today brief therapy is widely advertised at conferences, and insurance limitations have contributed to a briefer therapy.

Therapy focuses on the past vs. therapy focuses on the present. Traditional therapy examines the past while many contemporary therapists focus on the present. Many of us were trained in an ideology that says the past creates problems for clients because of

Directive Family Therapy
Published by The Haworth Press, Inc., 2007. All rights reserved.
doi:10.1300/5883_01

distressing memories and traumas. The assumption of traditional therapy has been that the past caused the present. Today we recognize that the *present* causes symptoms. This is the fundamental tenet of family therapy: Symptoms have a function in the present.

Negative unconscious vs. positive unconscious. What about the unconscious? The current perspective is that the unconscious should be viewed as a positive force rather than simply as a repository of awful and repressed thoughts. Dr. Erickson often said that if he misplaced something, he did not search for it because he knew his unconscious would find it. This is an extreme view of a positive unconscious that can lead clients to tap into their own creativity and trust their impulses.

Focus on the problem individual vs. focus on the problem in the social context. Most therapists continue to see individuals alone. In directive family therapy, the social context is the important element that is utilized to solve individual problems.

Focus on developing insight vs. focus on action. In traditional therapy the goal is to develop insight into the nature and history of the problem. The directive approach believes that insight does not necessarily lead to change; you do not need to share interpretations with clients.

Therapy is voluntary vs. therapy is compulsory. The change is from clients who want therapy to clients who don't want to be there but were offered a choice between therapy and jail; therapists do not want to be there under duress. The result is involuntary therapy.

Diagnosis is stressed vs. skills needed to change problems are stressed. Traditionalists focus on finding the correct diagnosis. Directive family therapists focus not on diagnostic labels, but on the skills needed to change symptoms.

Memories bring up the truth vs. memories can be false. Who could have predicted that the issue of false memories would someday threaten the influence of the past? Research indicates that past traumas can be remembered inaccurately or can even be illusions.

Evidence has shown that, with or without intention, therapists can implant false memories in a client (Yapko, 1994). Dr. Milton H. Erickson raised this issue by using hypnosis to deliberately change the memories and so the past of clients, in the case of the February Man (Haley, 1973).

Hypnosis is not respected vs. hypnosis is a valuable tool in psychotherapy. According to the World Health Organization, hypnosis is one of the most important adjuncts in psychotherapy. However, many therapists are not interested in acquiring the skills to practice it.

Psychosis and addiction are considered incurable vs. psychosis and addiction are considered curable. One double bind is to define a problem as incurable and then proceed to do therapy. The directive approach to therapy holds that people can change regardless of diagnosis and diagnosis should not interfere with the treatment.

Parents are blamed vs. parents are empowered and helpful. Instead of being critical of the parents and siding with the problem child, the directive approach seeks to establish a solid hierarchy with parents in charge of the rules of behavior.

Conversation cures vs. directives produce change. Conversation does not change people unless it prepares them to take action. Traditional therapy was nondirective and the field is still recovering from that stance. People can only change with direction or metaphor. Directive therapy tells people what to do, gives advice, and coaches them. If people do not do what you tell them to do, you need to work indirectly with metaphor. For example, if a man drinks and beats his wife, he can be told to stop. If he stops, a straightforward directive has worked. If he drinks and beats his wife harder than before, an indirect approach is needed. You can learn to apply directives in the relationships that you want to change.

I (J. H.) recall a meeting in the 1950s when behaviorists presented a new form of therapy. They decided that they could positively reinforce animals and also humans. One of the attendees said, "If you want a person to be emotional, you nod and smile. If they are not emotional, you do not react." A seasoned psychoanalyst replied indignantly, "It is immoral to direct someone outside of their awareness." The behaviorists said, "You do this anyhow." The analyst replied, "If you're doing it and you don't know you're doing it, it's okay." This is how some therapists feel about directives. They don't want you to tell people what to do but if you don't know you are directing, it is okay. You can't *not* give a directive. Directives give you something to talk about besides the past.

As an example, a mother brought her fifty-year-old son to Phoenix to Dr. Milton Erickson, who was doing a directive therapy. She said that her son would do nothing and that he constantly bothered her, not even leaving her alone to read a book. Erickson suggested that the mother drive the son out into the desert, stop the car, and push him out the door. Then she was to drive one mile and sit and read her book in the air-conditioned car while the son walked in the hot sun to catch up with her. The son would have no alternative except to walk. The mother was pleased with this task but the son was not. After some time, the son asked Erickson if he could not do some other exercise while his mother read her book. When he suggested that he would rather go bowling, Erickson agreed. With directives, you start by telling people what to do and then you back off while they decide what to do.

Straightforward directives include giving advice, coaching, ordeals, and penance. Directives do not start with giving a directive but by establishing a trusting relationship so that the client will do what you say. Directives start with saying hello, being empathetic, being concerned, all of which encourage people to want to do what you say. You can coach a wife to win back her husband or coach adolescents to improve their relationship with their parents. An ordeal is when you direct someone to do something that is harder on them than the symptom and they give up the symptom (Haley, 1984).

Another straightforward directive is penance. You give the client a penance that is helpful to others while at the same time effective in alleviating the client's feelings of guilt over something he or she did.

Indirect directives can be used when therapists lack power in a situation. Examples of indirect directives are restraining people from changing—advising them to remain the same—and so imposing a paradox; metaphoric communication; absurd tasks; and doing nothing, in which case the client may feel that he or she must do something.

Paradox is considered manipulative vs. paradox is legitimate. Paradox is curious as a technique in therapy. Symptoms can be encouraged deliberately to get rid of them. Another form of paradox is to restrain the client from improving. This can have the curious effect of clients pulling you to change rather than you pulling them. Paradox is at the heart of all therapy in the sense that the therapist must direct the client to change spontaneously.

Privacy vs. observation. Another change in therapy has been in regard to secrecy. Traditional therapists keep the interchange behind closed doors. Now training takes place in rooms equipped with one-way mirrors so that therapists and clients can be observed. Exposure to therapy ideas is everywhere—on television, radio, and the Internet. Therapy in groups represents a major change in the field.

Full exploration of cultural background vs. minimization of culture. Erickson said that every therapist should study anthropology to become familiar with the diversity of backgrounds of both clients and therapists. However, the exploration of cultural roots is similar to the analysis of the past practiced by traditional therapists. Since we cannot be experts in all cultures, the position of directive therapy is to focus on the structural similarities of what people have in common that lead to change or resolution of a particular problem. Exploration of cultural differences often prolongs therapy unnecessarily. Courtesy and respect are the necessary elements (Richeport-Haley, 1998a, 1998b, 2001).

Traditional Therapy	Directive Therapy
Long-term therapy	Brief therapy
Therapy focuses on the past	Therapy focuses on the present
Negative unconscious	Positive unconscious
Focus on the problem individual	Focus on the problem in the social context
Focus on developing insight	Focus on action
Therapy is voluntary	Therapy is compulsory
Diagnosis is stressed	Skills needed to change problems are stressed
Memories bring up the truth	Memories can be false
Hypnosis is not respected	Hypnosis is a valuable tool in psychotherapy
Psychosis and addiction are considered incurable	Psychosis and addiction are considered curable
Parents are blamed	Parents are empowered and helpful
Conversation cures	Directives produce change

Paradox is considered manipulative	Paradox is legitimate
Privacy	Observation
Full exploration of cultural background	Minimization of culture

STAGES OF FAMILY LIFE

Problems and symptoms don't occur randomly in life; they cluster. Often they coincide with our biological development and social changes as we move from one stage in the life cycle to the next. One example is when children have trouble disengaging from their parents and leaving home, which occurs in most families. In many societies, becoming an adult is accompanied by a formal ritual, often tied to religion. Often, however, we slip from one stage of development to the next without even noticing it. One goal of therapy is to work through the difficult problems that occur at different life stages when no rituals are available to help ease the transition. Haley developed this framework in writing *Uncommon Therapy* (1973) to present the therapy of Dr. Milton Erickson. There are transitions from birth, to infancy, to childhood, to school, to adolescence, to leaving home, to being a parent, to being a grandparent, to dealing with old age. Often people become blocked at one of these stages and must be helped beyond it. Usually a symptom indicates a stage-of-life problem and guides a therapist to an approach.

A case illustrates how moving on to the next stage can normalize the problem. I (J. H.) had a case of a young woman with a trembling right hand. It shook irregularly and neurological tests failed to show a physical cause. The woman was referred to me for hypnosis. I asked her what would happen if the problem got worse.

She said, "I'll lose my job." I asked, "And what if you lose your job?" She said with a sigh, "My husband will have to go to work." The parents protested their daughter's supporting the husband and tried to break up the marriage. The woman became pregnant and stopped working, and her husband had to go to work to support the family. The parents who wanted her back home didn't want her back with a baby. They began to support the marriage instead of tearing it down. This happened in the natural stages of becoming independent. The couple went from one life stage—marriage—to another life stage—the birth of a child, which in this case normalized the problem.

Serious problems may result from someone entering into a family, such as in childbirth, or moving out of a family, such as leaving home. When children attend school, they begin their disengagement from the family. Next is adolescence, which is the most ambiguous stage. It is halfway between being at home as a child and leaving home as an adult. The ultimate goal is to live outside the home and support oneself. A child may have many functions in the family that change when the threat of leaving home arises. There are different stages of leaving home, and some are positive. But problems often occur, as when a child leaves home after being a bridge between the parents and others in the family for many years. The dynamics change when a space is created in the house by a child leaving home. The therapist may face an upset child and upset parents watching their child leave. *As an example, when I (J. H.) was doing research on family relationships, I was looking for a normal family to try out a test. A neighbor volunteered. On the day the family was supposed to come for the test, they called and said they were no longer a normal family. Their daughter was going off to college and the house was in chaos.*

Directive Family Therapy will help you to identify problems clearly and make and carry out a plan to change people. You will surprise yourself by using the directive techniques in this book. Many students have asked Haley what they should do with such and such a problem. This book is a response to that question. Of the thousands of cases he has seen personally, supervised* over the years, or discussed in conversations with Dr. Milton Erickson, the cases in this book are some of our favorite teaching examples for clearly illustrating directives to resolve problems.

---

*Directive therapy requires active directive live supervision, which has eveloved over the years with changing technology. Many of the cases in this book were supervised live and filmed behind a one-way mirror with Jay Haley either calling the trainee out of the room for consultation, giving suggestions to the trainee by telephone, or more recently, giving suggestions on a computer monitor where the therapist could see the messages while the client could not (Scherl & Haley, 2000). These methods are not mutually exclusive.

Chapter 1

How to Be a Wise Child

Witnessing an infant waving an arm, one recognizes that he or she must learn this action. A child begins life as a helpless being. An infant who comes into the world has surprises waiting. Children are wise. They have to learn many complicated aspects of becoming human.

This is a more complex process than people realize, unless they find an infant who will teach them. As we learn from Dr. Milton H. Erickson, infants have the beginnings of sex drives, but they are not apprehensive about it. This chapter explores aspects of infant and adolescent biological and sexual development for the purpose of illustrating the process humans go through to learn to become fully functioning adults. It will also be useful in cases with men and women who are apprehensive about sex and want to do something about any malfunctioning. *I (J. H.) was a student of Dr. Erickson before he was famous. These ideas were expressed in one of our audiotaped conversations (Haley & Richeport, 1991a). At the time and to this day I have never seen a better presentation of the infancy and development of human beings and the people involved with them. I memorized it and told it to many clients. It is unique because it is presented from the point of view of the infant.* The original sequences and phrasing of Dr. Erickson's conversational style have been retained to demonstrate his ability to work on many therapeutic levels at once. Subheads have been added for clarity and the text of the monologue presented here is an abridged version of the original.

Directive Family Therapy
Published by The Haworth Press, Inc., 2007. All rights reserved.
doi:10.1300/5883_02

DEVELOPMENT OF THE CHILD

How are you going to have a normal, well-adjusted person, unless they can look at you, and at other things, with that same sense of self-confidence that the little baby does? The little baby knows that it's a nice baby, a good baby, a bright baby, an intelligent baby, a competent baby, isn't that right? And therefore it has a good opinion of itself. It knows it can pick up that toy and rattle it. Too many adults do not know that they can pick up that toy and rattle it. They're thinking what will other people think, what will they say, how do they feel about it. When a baby picks it up it rattles because it knows it's a good baby and it can make a good noise.

Now what I have to tell you already know—and yet you haven't organized it. In the first place, how does one learn things? The baby starts life in a certain position, arms flexed, hands closed, and it has to start from scratch to learn every possible thing. It's got no background, memory, or experience. So the baby flexes its arm; it does not extend its arm—it's quite a job to learn how to extend its arm. The flexor muscles get tired, and the extensor muscles take over and extend the arm, just to relieve the fatigue of the flexor muscles. The baby learns to extend its arm, to move the shoulder; it learns the elbow movements, shoulder movements first. Then it learns eventually by trial and error to open the hand. It can close it reflexively, but to open the hand deliberately. The last movement learned in the arm is of course the wrist movement. It learns the pronation and supination movements of the arm later as a deliberate thing. But that's a function of the use of the hand. The same way with the matter of eyesight. The baby has to look at this, look at that, and there is countless repetition of its looks. No matter how good a retina it has, it has to look at red and blue and green and yellow many times before it acquires the experience of yellowness or greenness. And it has to make many errors in the process of learning colors accurately. In all of its sensory experience, all of its motor experience, there's endless repetition. But the baby is under a handicap because its body is changing in size all the time. The mere fact that you've got a full complement of muscles, joints, bones, nerves, and organs doesn't mean anything. A perfectly developed person who sits down to a computer the first time doesn't know how to type, because they know nothing about the sequences and patterns of finger movements. Furthermore, they don't know finger sensations in typing. They have to learn that the little finger has to hit a key relatively harder than the four fingers in order to get an even touch. They learn an even touch on a typewriter by measuring the unevenness of the touch of the individual fingers, because there's different strength in the fingers. And so they use muscles to varying degrees to get that even touch. If you tried to learn typing and one day the typewriter keyboard was one size, and the next day it was another size, the next day it was another, it would be a fearful handicap. And any expert stenographer who sits down to a keyboard twice the usual size is an amateur. And yet the growing child has to learn how to put its hand to its mouth.

Now I think you probably know this matter of increment in stimulation. A baby learns to put its hand into its mouth. The arm grows longer, and when there is sufficient extension in the growth of the arm, then the baby can't put his hand in his mouth, the increment is so great. So he has to learn it all over again. And all the learning is in that pattern. People recognize that exercise is good for the muscles. Actually exercise is good for all forms of body behavior. It's tremendously important to hear a distant sound, a near sound, a sound up above, a sound below, behind, just to exercise the ears. The same is true of vision. One needs to exercise the eyes. When you actually recognize that, then you can recognize the tremendous importance of exercising the genitals, too. The little baby is exercising the eyes by looking at red, blue, yellow, and green repetitiously. And it needs to do it in a repetitious fashion. The baby is learning to recognize eyes, ears, nose, mouth, hair, but the parents throw a fit if it touches its genitals. Yet the genitals are as important as the eyes, and ears, and nose. You couldn't very

well learn to type if, every time you touched the letter A or the letter B you got a frowning look and were made to feel guilty. You've
got to learn the entire body if you're going to live in a normal way.
The learning of the body means the learning of all parts of the
body. You can't really learn to write with your right hand without
learning in part how to write with your left hand. Nobody is ever
trained to write with their feet, and yet any normal adult can put a
pencil between his toes and scrawl his name better than he could
the first time he tried to write his name with his right hand. Because there is a transfer of learning from one part of the body to
another, certain parts of the body become dominant, but it's so tremendously important when you learn to write to learn something
with your feet at the same time, a part of that writing. And you'll
see the little child trying to write twist its mouth, wiggle its hand,
squirm with its entire body, shuffle its feet, until it has learned to
localize writing movements in the hand and the arm.

Learning Body Parts

Now a little baby hasn't learned where its ear is until it can
reach up with its right hand and touch its right ear, reach up with its
left hand and touch its left ear. But it still hasn't learned until it can
take its left hand and touch its right hand, and then touch the left
ear with the right hand. But it still hasn't learned where its ears are,
and how the ears feel, until it can touch the opposite ear by reach-
ing behind its head. Then and only then does a child really know
where its ears are. And it has to learn the body in that particular
fashion. By discovering all parts of its body.

How Does the Child Learn to Say "Mama"?

It accidentally makes the "Mama" noise and receives approval,
but it's a chance thing. It utters more sounds and accidentally says
"Mama" again. It gets rewarded by attention, but the child hasn't

learned to say "Mama" until it says "Mama" in the bedroom, in the crib, on the floor, on top of the big bed, in the closet, in the hall, in the living room, in the kitchen, out on the front porch, out in the front yard, in every conceivable place. And the child says "Mama" indiscriminately to Mother, Father, Brother, Sister. It hasn't learned to say "Mama" until it says "Mama" to Mother and Mother alone. And then it has an utterly bewildering experience. The neighbor woman comes over with a baby the same age. They recognize each other as infants do. Each has learned to say "Mama" to Mother. And then they have the horrifyingly shocking experience to see this other good citizen saying "Mama" to the wrong person, and not until then have they really learned to whom to say "Mama." And they've got to have control of the utterance "Mama" no matter where they are. And so it's a learning process, a repetitious process.

Now the child has to learn to urinate.

Toilet Training

Mother wants to toilet train the baby. What experience does the baby have? It doesn't even know what urination is; it doesn't even know what part of the body. Because a pat on the belly to a baby feels the same as a pat on the back, pat on the thigh, pat on the head. It hasn't got the experiential background to say "That was a pat on my abdomen." When it gets a full bladder, reflexively it releases the sphincter. And the baby gets an experience of a warm, wet feeling without knowing what a warm, wet feeling is. But through repetition the child discovers that sooner or later, without a concept of time, that that warm, wet feeling is going to be followed by a cold wet feeling. Mother's tried to teach the baby toilet habits, but that's too soon. Because Baby can't really learn toilet habits until it completes that concept of learning. And when Baby is really ready to learn toilet habits, Baby's sitting on the living room floor. And all of a sudden Baby looks around with a wondering, questioning look. It has suddenly become aware of pelvic pressure. The intelligent mother says Baby is ready to wet and she rushes the baby into the bathroom. And the baby is ready to learn toilet habits. But not until the child learns that unlocated sensation of pelvic pressure can the child learn toilet habits. All right. Now all of this learning, whether it's visual, auditory, urinary, whatever it is, takes place in small fragments here and there in a mixed-up fashion. I'm trying to present it to you one idea at a time. Has the child learned to urinate by being placed on the toilet? It really hasn't. The child has the difficult task of learning to urinate by itself. So Mother has to teach it when it gets that pelvic pressure to pick up one foot and put it down, pick up the other foot and put it down, headed for the bathroom. And eventually the child learns that. At first the child does not allow sufficient time to get from the living room to the bathroom. Finally it learns that. Then it goes to the kitchen. It has to learn geography all over again; the kitchen is further away than the living room. But the child finally masters that, then it goes out in the backyard and arrives at the bathroom too late; it wets its pants—it didn't know about geographical distance and the time involved. Finally it learns to allow sufficient time to get to the bathroom. And it rushes from the backyard into the bathroom in adequate time, and some confounded adult is in there. And the child wets its pants not because it resents the adult being there, but because the allowance of time is insufficient. And so the child wets its pants. It's had a tremendously important elementary lesson, and we all have to learn things at an elementary level. The child discovers the adult is in the bathroom, wets its pants, has received an elementary lesson, a profoundly important elementary lesson, that is, in your own physiological functioning you've got to respect the physiological functioning of other people. It's utterly, completely necessary for that fundamental lesson to be learned. And yet what do mothers do? They spank the child because it wets its pants, and interfere with the learning of that lesson. And yet the child eventually learns to allow for the bathroom to be occupied. And then it really has a consideration, but not an intellectually formulated conception of the rights and privileges and needs of others. One item I omitted concerns the little boy who has learned toilet habits; he allows plenty of time for distance, for the bathroom being occupied, and Sunday morning his mother dresses him up in a brand-new suit. And then she hurriedly dresses, and the son wets his pants. And the reason is not anger toward the mother or anything of that sort; he doesn't know where his penis is in relationship to his new suit. It's the first time he's had it on. And he's as helpless as you are when you borrow a friend's car, different model, different make, different dashboard, and you're driving along, and finally you discover it's time to turn on the lights. Now where, where is that light button? You hunt and hunt and hunt. Not because you want to drive recklessly without lights, but because you don't know where the light button is. The little boy in a brand-new suit has not explored it, and his mother doesn't want wet pants. She'd better send him to the toilet right away and tell him to try to urinate, and thus he discovers relative positions, and then when he has to urinate he's already explored it, and he doesn't wet his pants. And the spanking he got for wetting his pants was his mother's oversight, not his antagonism because she's taken away his old suit and forced him into a new suit; he's just unfamiliar. But the child hasn't really learned to urinate because urination is something that's not only going to occur in the bathroom, it's got to occur in other parts of the world. At first the little boy—and I use a little boy because that's easier to visualize and to understand—has been toilet trained; he wants to stand up and make bubbles like Daddy. He stands up there bravely and sprays the bathroom. Until he learns to direct the stream of urine into the toilet bowl, then he can make bubbles like Daddy, but there's more involved there. He's learned a fundamental, elementary lesson in controlling the direction and the use of his penis. And it's a very simple, elementary level, but he'd better learn how to direct the use of his penis at that simple level that he can understand. When he can direct it into the toilet bowl and use it for the pleasurable purpose of creating bubbles like Daddy. Then the next step the child has to learn is, you urinate in the toilet bowl—but the boy if he is ever going to mature has got to be able to urinate out in the backyard, he's got to urinate on the tree, the flower bed, the lawn mower, the dog, the cat, through a hole in the fence. In other words, as far as he can conceive of the world he's got to be able to urinate—in any part of the world where he needs to. And so he tries it out, just as the baby tries out saying "Mama" in the closet, under the bed, on top of a chair, behind the davenport, in order to have control of the utterance of "Mama." The little boy explores the external world. But that fundamental learning that's so important. What does a boy have to do? He has to be able to use his penis in the outside world, not just in the parental home. He's got to have a sense of freedom, a sense of mastery, a sense of confidence in his penis.

SEXUAL PLEASURE

All right. The little boy ought to be proud of his penis when he urinates on the dog, on the tree, on the lawn mower, the flower bed; he can really use that organ of his. And to put it through a hole in the fence and urinate through it. He doesn't really know what he's doing, but at a very elementary level he's learning to put his penis someplace and derive satisfaction, comfort, and pleasure. He can put it in a bottle, he can put it in a tin can, there's no way of explaining anything to him at his age, anything at all about ejaculation or a vagina. That's way beyond his powers of comprehension, just as much as you do not teach cube root to the kindergarten child who's trying to master one plus one. It's just plain idiotic to teach that child struggling with one and one and two and two, what cube root is.

All right. I had a delightful experience on one occasion with one of my sons. He was being undressed to go to bed, and in the nude he started racing around the room. And in doing so he happened in swinging his arms to strike himself on the buttocks. And he stopped and looked around to see who was behind him, who had hit him. He looked puzzled, but with the short attention span of infancy, he soon lost interest in that and continued racing. So every night I had him in the nude racing around. He slapped his fanny again and stopped to look. Then one night it happened again and he sat down and examined the back of his calves. He looked at the front of his legs, then he twisted his body so he could see the back of his calves, then he felt on the back of his thighs, and tried to see them. The next night—it was a rather orderly progression—he slapped his fanny, he sat down, he examined the calves, the front of his legs, the front of his thighs, the back of his thighs, his fanny, and he felt the lumbar region of his back. Lost interest. The next night he did the same thing, and reached up in back of his shoulders and happened to touch the back of his head. A dawning comprehension. He had known for a long time that he had a back of his head, that the back of his head was behind his eyes, that he couldn't see, therefore this was a part of his body he could feel but not see, and then he felt of his shoulders, felt of his back, felt of his fanny, and then looked at the back of his calves again. Then he knew that this body of his was not only a body he could see and feel, but also a body he could feel and not see. And that dawning comprehension, and he really felt of his body, front and back, then he went and got his footstool, put it in the middle of the room, went to the other side of the room and backed up. He knew where his fanny was and he sat squarely on the stool, instead of sitting on it too soon, off to one side, or too far over. He knew where his fanny was, he could aim it. One of the most beautiful demonstrations of the verification that he knew where that part of his body that he could feel and not see but still could use accurately. And you watch little children as they learn how to sit on a stool, and how they feel of their bottom, and try to recognize it as the part you feel but don't see, and it differs so much from the part you feel and see. And a little bit later we gave Robert a taste of a new food. He didn't know whether he liked it. So he took another taste—and stood up to taste it. Took another, and lay down on the floor to taste it. Then he shut one eye and tasted it, went out to the living room and tasted it there. Went out on the back porch and tasted it there. He tasted it in all conceivable situations and wound up by deciding he really liked it. But it was such a laborious, but comprehensive way of learning to like it. Lying on his belly, lying on his back, eyes shut, one eye shut, and tasting it, a thoroughly searching way of tasting a food.

Self-Touching

Now when it comes to becoming aware of the genitals, the child plays with his genitals and his big toes and his ear and his nose indiscriminately. I like to simplify it for patients by stating that there are three sets of nerves to the penis, then I illustrate that they have one kind of feeling in their scalp, and they test it this way (with a pencil), not with their fingertips because then they get confused with the fingertips and the scalp feeling, then they touch the eyeball, another sensation, they touch the tongue, or the lip. It's all touch, it's different sensations. They can look at red, that's one sensation, yellow, that's another sensation, the paper is identical. But the quality of the color is different. That there are three sets of nerves to the penis, one set for the skin, one set for the shaft, and one for the glans penis. And of course neurologically speaking that is correct. But it's much more involved than that; that's only a simplification. The child better learn all the sensations of the skin of the penis, because the pronouncement "I now pronounce you man and wife" doesn't tell him anything at all about the skin of the penis sensations. "I pronounce you graduate, therefore you can take this computer, you've got a full complement of nerves and muscles and joints, and you can type." No. It doesn't work. You have to learn. So the child plays with his penis. He plays with his big toe in order to find out where it really is, and to tell the difference between the right big toe and the left big toe. He has to learn how to get an erection, how to lose it, just as the newlywed had to learn when and how to get an erection. So the little boy plays with his penis. Little children can be born with an erection, it serves no use. The little boy in the boy's camp, he's a pain in the neck to the counselor, he gets a full bladder, he gets an erection, he can't urinate. And the counselor wearily puts him back to bed and wishes the little boy would grow up. The boy has to learn the skin of the penis, he has to learn the shaft, the head of the penis. And go through as much exploratory activity with his genitals as he does with his eyes and ears. Then he has to learn that he can get an erection, he's got to learn how to lose it, his span of attention is short, he starts it and doesn't finish it, but he has to keep on repeating that behavior until finally he can actually get an erection and then lose interest and lose it, and then get it back, and then lose it again. He's got to learn the difference between a flaccid penis and the skin sensations then, a semi-erect penis and the skin sensations at that stage, and the skin sensations at full erection. And the sensations of the shaft of the penis, very similarly. Because what does the psychiatrist get in his office: the man who is impotent, psychologically impotent, and he doesn't know the feeling of the skin of the penis, he doesn't know the feelings of the shaft, he doesn't know the feeling of the head of the penis. Is he trying to spite his mother, has he got some incest complex, or is he just plain ignorant, as he often is. Now you can drive an Austin car, you can park it, parallel parking, angle parking, you can turn the corner, you can back it up and turn it around. And you're an expert in traffic anywhere. Then you get into a Cadillac. You better learn how to parallel-park it, how to back it up, how to turn a corner. You may be an expert with an Austin; with a Cadillac you're somewhat of an amateur. Then you get into a great big truck and you start learning to drive all over again. The little boy has a penis of such and such a size, with such and such–sized hands. He's constantly changing from Austin to Cadillac, and he's got to get new learnings with each increment of size. Also, you can recognize that veal comes from the same species of animal that beefsteak comes from. It's a different consistency, it's a different tissue, different flavor, everything's different. The veal doesn't seem to be related to beefsteak; it's just young beefsteak, very young. The boy is a growing creature, and at puberty he starts to change from veal to beefsteak. He'd better learn all of his learnings all over again, because he's using a different kind of tissue, with a different consistency, with a different development. At puberty the boy really has to relearn his previous understandings, so at puberty the boy has to engage in a good deal of genital play.

Ejaculation

At puberty the boy's skin changes, he gets a new floor for his genitals, he gets pubic hair, he gets carpet. He better relearn his genital understandings pretty thoroughly—the size is changing, the relative relationships, because his arms are longer, his legs are longer, his body is relatively shorter, and he really needs to learn things thoroughly, and so he has that increased activity. But of course that isn't all there is to it. Because at puberty he has to learn how to have an ejaculation; what is an ejaculation? You can think of it as the expulsion of sexual fluid. But actually to simplify it, you can divide it into urethral fluid, prostatic fluid, and seminiferous fluid. And he'd better have it in a one-two-three order. This little baby being given solid food for the first time doesn't digest it. It swallows the solid food and goes into the stomach and passes out into the intestine, and a half hour too late the salivary glands start secreting, but they're not going to digest that food, it's down in the small intestine already. Too late the stomach starts to secrete, but the food isn't there, it's passed on down to the lower bowel. The child has to learn with the ingestion of solid food in its mouth to start the parada gland, the submaxillary, sublingual, mucosa, into secreting immediately. And then the esophageal glands, and then the glands in the upper end of the stomach, the middle of the stomach, lower end of the stomach, so that it goes in a one-two-three order all the way through the gastrointestinal tract. Then he can digest his food.

But you respect the individual capacity to learn. One of my sons learned to digest beans very readily, but he was six years old before his GI tract learned how to digest peas, and actually which are more digestible? To his gastrointestinal tract beans were more digestible than peas, so his GI tract just simply didn't learn to digest peas.

At puberty the boy has to learn to get his urethral secretion, his prostatic secretion, his seminiferous. And he's got to have it in a one-two-three order. And to get it rapidly enough so it sounds like, or feels like, just one thing. Now you cannot get physiologically satisfied when your food passes through the stomach undigested. You do not get physiological satisfaction unless you get the benefits of first the urethral, second the prostatic, and third the seminiferous. At first the boy has a seminiferous ejaculation, or a urethral, or a prostatic, and then he'll have a combination of two. All of the various permutations of ABC. Until eventually he manages to get it always ABC, ABC. How many times does he have to have an ejaculation? Whatever number of times is requisite to coming up with ABC or one-two-three.

I get some of these men as patients. I can think of a doctor who had been married for about ten years, fathered a couple of children, never had enjoyed intercourse. I tried to give him this lecture. He said "I went to medical school, too." "Maybe you did, maybe you better wear a condom and take your specimen down to the office and tell me what you think about it." He took some eleven specimens down. No consistency. Too fluid on one occasion, to viscous on another occasion. The sperm count was too large on another, and too low on another. There was too much prostatic fluid on one occasion, not enough prostatic fluid on another occasion. And he came back and said, "I may have gone to medical school, but I didn't learn anything about sexual functioning." My therapy for him was, lock yourself in the bathroom—because he had a history of having masturbated only twice; both times his father caught him before he completed the act, and lectured him, and made him promise never, never, never to touch himself. And he fought with himself throughout the rest of his development and never touched himself. It was a horrible temptation when with his wife, because he did get an erection, but he didn't dare touch himself. And they were pronounced man and wife and he still didn't know how to enjoy sex relations. So he locked himself in the bathroom, and he indulged in all the erotic thinking, made use of his medical knowledge to sense the feel of the corpus callosum, and everything else about his penis. He paid attention to the sensations in the glans penis, the shaft, the skin, the foreskin, to the base of the penis, the feeling of the urethra. I told him to do it every day or every other day for a month. One day he was headed for the bathroom, had a sudden change of mind, picked his wife up, put her on the bed, and proceeded to have intercourse, the first time he'd ever enjoyed intercourse with his wife. She was also my patient. She promptly came over for a special appointment to tell me that she had enjoyed intercourse, because he was functioning right. But he learned it by acquiring the learnings in a blind fashion. The way he should have acquired it as a kid at puberty, as an early teenager, as a late teenager.

Giving and Receiving Sexual Pleasure

Now once the boy learns to have an ejaculation, have it in the right order, have it in a satisfying way, he's still got a deuce of a lot to learn. Because he's got to learn the very very difficult thing of giving and receiving sexual pleasure. From whom would you learn that? The boy who is seeking sexual knowledge tries to find somebody who talks his language. Not how many ribbons can you put in a dress, but how many home runs can you bat? And all the other boy language. Can you wrassle, can you jump? Not what shade of color goes with this, and how do you do your hair? That's alien language, it's offensive language. So he seeks out other boys. He's got to learn how to give and how to receive sexual pleasure from someone else. And so at a very elementary level he exchanges views on whether or not their penises are identical, shaped the same, because you've got to identify with someone else.

Boys size up each other's muscles. They size up each other's ability to jump, to play ball, and they size up the ability of the other chap to have an ejaculation. And how far can you shoot when you come. And they handle each other. Now how do they handle each other? Sometimes manually. Sometimes by observing it. Sometimes by hearing about it. Is that the homosexual stage, or is it a fundamental, elementary level of learning how to give and to receive sexual pleasure in relationship to another person? And you'd better start with somebody that uses your language than some alien creature who talks another kind of language entirely. Who's got an alien body, can't play ball, can't wrassle, can't do anything interesting, hasn't even got muscles.

The boy goes through what the psychoanalyst calls the homosexual stage. I think it's a stupid term, because they aren't homosexual, they're just learning the vocabulary. And so they go through that learning process. Now all these learnings don't develop separately. The boy has to learn how to produce an ejaculation in himself by manual stimulation, friction, and so on. He's got to be aware of the fact that other boys do. But to be mature and be a man, he's got to make provision for emotional values. And so he develops wet dreams. At first those dreams are pretty vague. He sleeps quietly, doesn't touch himself, but in relationship to ideas and thoughts and feelings he gets an erection and he has a wet dream, he has an ejaculation. He has to have enough ejaculations, enough wet dreams, so that in his wet dreams his response to feelings, thoughts, dream images, he can have a correct ejaculation. And of course Mother says he's abusing himself, and his learning is impeded. He's not having those wet dreams to spite his mother, he's having those wet dreams because physiologically he's learning something. Organizing actual physical experience with concepts of feelings and experiences and memories and ideas. Vague, it's true, but nevertheless very vital to him.

I covered this matter of learning from someone who spoke your own language, who could communicate with you, and with whom you could communicate understandably.

Sexual development doesn't occur in an orderly manner of units. The first elementary lesson, that girls are good for stimulating mucous membranes, for giving satisfaction to the inner man. As I watch my sons in their dealings with girls, yes—Burt would take Yvonne and they'd go and buy a hot dog with plenty of relish and catsup, and I don't know what all, on that hot dog at Mike's place, and sit there starry-eyed enjoying mucous membrane stimulation in the company of someone of the opposite sex. Having downed the hot dog, they'd wander down the street and get a hamburger with relish and pickles and onions and catsup on the hamburger. They sit there starry-eyed again enjoying mucous membrane stimulation in each other's company. Then of course they learn to roller-skate, where in a way they learn to engage in pleasurable, rhythmical, physical activity with one another and they culminate that in mucous membrane stimulation at the Dairy Queen. Then they go swimming, and top it off with mucous membrane stimulation. Then the slow, gradual discovery that girls could dance. And go hiking. And then the discovery that Yvonne was really bright. She was brilliant in history and she was a whiz at math. She was really tops. She could enjoy a hot dog and a hamburger, and she could really skate, but she was a whiz at math. The discovery was that a girl had other qualities than purely physical.

The boy has to learn all of those things at the elementary level, and as they learn that, and as they observe their elders, what is a girl, and all that crude coarse talk that is so condemned. They crudely wonder about the girls, their hips, their breasts, and their willingness to pinch a girl on the buttocks, and to accidentally bump her breast with their hand or their elbow. Until they have really located the breasts so that they can help a girl put on a sweater and then draw a hand over it, but first they poked it with their elbow, or bumped it. The crude searching for the location. The crude bumping of buttocks with a girl, the crude slapping, and their crude talk. Because they lack the language of refinement, and the language of emotional regard. They have to confirm their own observations of others, and so you have those bull sessions in which sex is mentioned, and their instinctual drives keep forcing them to make further and further extensions.

And the first love affair. The girl is put upon a pedestal, and kept there, and looked at and worshipped from afar, because they're not sufficiently familiar with the opposite sex to dare to let her be too close. She is a strange creature. They keep the girl on the pedestal until she shows clay feet. And they erect another pedestal for another girl, but this time it's not so high, until that girl shows clay feet. Until finally the girl and the boy meet on a level where they can actually look at each other straight in the eye without the boy craning the neck. But of course the girls put the boys on pedestals until they show clay feet. And everything the boy does the girl does in her own way.

The boy has to speculate on what kissing is. My eleven-year-old knows what kissing is. It's disgusting. He wonders when he'll ever degenerate to that. And he means that. But when he is speculating on when he is going to degenerate to that, he's also recognizing the fact that he will achieve that. But at the present time it's a mark of degeneration.

How do boys and girls actually learn about sex itself? By that time they have enough general understanding, so they can seek out information from books, from elders, from trusted people, and they can correlate it, without necessarily experimenting. A certain number of boys just cannot correlate and synthesize their information, and they go in for experimentation. Necking from the neck up, from the waist up, from the waist down, depending on their general—if you want to call it that—moral background. So do some girls have to learn by actual experimentation.

I can think of a young girl who came to me for this discussion. Her father was a doctor and he sent her to me. The father was a patient of mine also. It was a delight to give this discussion to the girl. She listened, and then I discussed this matter of how girls learn about sex. She says, "Suppose I tell you how I learned about it, and you see if I fit into the normal category." She says, "I have been necking from the neck up. I knew that someday I'd get married, I knew my father was a doctor, I knew he was your patient, I knew that when I got engaged that I could come to you and have you tell me everything I needed to know about sex. What I needed to know about my breasts and my hips and my genitals. So I just went in for heavy kissing. I learned what it was to have a tongue inside my mouth, and I wondered what a penis inside my vagina would feel like. And so I did French kissing while I thought about a penis inside my vagina. And I liked the tongue in my mouth, I like kissing, I like sloppy kissing, where his lips would get all wet and mine would get all wet. I wanted him to feel my breasts, but I didn't know how much control I had. So I told him I didn't know how much control I had and would he please not—and when he did put his hand on my breast I slapped his hand and told him I meant it." Now that was an awfully innocent girl, with a rather rigid family background. But her willingness to correlate the tongue in her mouth and the penis in her vagina indicated the fearlessness of her thinking. She was an awfully naïve, innocent girl, but not the least bit afraid to think. And how many girls now and boys are terrified at the thought of thinking those things.

Sexual Differences Between Men and Women

There is another consideration that is so often overlooked in the biological development of an individual. A man can have sexual relations with a woman; it is biologically a local performance. The sperm cells are secreted, and once that process has been completed, the manufacture of the sperm cells, of the man's body has no longer any use for that. They serve no purpose to him; they are useful only when the man gets rid of them by depleting them in the vagina. A man's sexual performance biologically is a purely local phenomena, and can be accomplished very quickly in the space of seconds. It's just local, and once he has deposited the sperm cells he's all through with the sexual act. Biologically speaking, when a woman has intercourse, to complete that single act of intercourse biologically, she becomes pregnant. That lasts for nine months. She lactates; that lasts another six months. Then she has the problem of caring for the child, teaching it, feeding it, looking after it, and enabling it to grow up. And for a woman the single act of intercourse, in our culture, takes about eighteen years to complete. A man—eighteen seconds is all that is necessary. How is a woman's body built? Very few people stop to realize it, how completely a woman's body enters into the sexual relationship.

When a woman starts having an active, thoroughly well-adjusted sexual life, the calcium of her skeleton changes. The count, the calcium count increases. Her foot gets about a quarter of a size larger, eyebrow ridges increase a little bit. The angle of her jaw shifts, the chin is a little bit heavier, the nose a trifle longer, there's likely to be a change in her hair, her breasts change in either size or consistency or both. The hips, mons veneris change either in size or in consistency. The shape of the spine alters a bit. The circulation of the blood to the breasts and through the thyroid changes. So physiologically and physically the girl changes in as short a time as two weeks of ardent lovemaking. Because biologically her body has to be prepared to take care of another creature for nine long months inside, and then, for months and years afterwards with all her body behavior centering around her offspring. With each child there's a tendency for a woman's feet to get larger, the angle of her jaw to change. Every pregnancy brings about these tremendous physical and physiological changes. A man doesn't grow more whiskers because he's having intercourse, he doesn't alter his calcium count any, he doesn't enlarge his feet. He doesn't change his center of gravity one bit. It is a local affair with him. But intercourse and pregnancy is a tremendous biological, physiological alteration for a woman. She has to enter it as a complete physical being.

Chapter 2

Birth

WENDY THE WEEPER

When Wendy began weeping, her relatives and friends were surprised. It was her first birth and it had been relatively easy for her to reach this stage of motherhood. Her husband, Sammy, was irritated with her because he had work to do and the birth interfered with it. He was a reluctant father. When her doctor heard she was weeping, he was surprised and came in to cheer her up. He had seen many mothers who were depressed after delivery. He expected to discharge her to take the baby home, but he could not when she was weeping so severely. After a few days they had to discharge her from the hospital because they needed the space. When she was finally discharged, she wept as if she didn't belong anywhere. This might have been because she did not know where to go with the baby. The couple decided to close up their home and take the baby home to the husband's parents' house since she didn't seem ready to go to her own house. Because Wendy was weeping so much she said she could not take care of the baby in their own house.

Wendy was puzzled as to why she was so sad after giving birth. She became depressed to the point of weeping all day after the birth. Her in-laws called her weeping postpartum depression. This made her officially a "mental health problem." Her mother-in-law was troubled by her condition and said "I'm not sure I want my

Directive Family Therapy
Published by The Haworth Press, Inc., 2007. All rights reserved.
doi:10.1300/5883_03

grandchild raised by a "mental case." Her father-in-law was willing to have her in their home while she recuperated. Having
Wendy in the house weeping was a cause of conflict. The mother-
in-law thought that her husband should not be so involved with his
daughter-in-law, which raised questions about their relationship.
Wendy's husband was irritated with her because she was interfer-
ing with his work and he was relieved to have her occupied with
his parents. Her doctor was pleased that she would go home to her
in-laws' house because she was a manic-depressive. He tried to
jolly her out of the weeping without success. With the husband's
lack of interest in Wendy's distress, and his impatience with her,
he did not notice that her mental state was resulting in her isolation
from a support system. She had friends who were not visiting her
because they knew she was upset and had a mental health problem,
so she felt alone when she came out of the hospital. Her in-laws
were exasperated with her weeping. Everyone was ready to expect
difficulties even though she began to take care of the baby while
protesting she couldn't take care of the baby. The family did not
know that many new mothers experience depression ranging from
the blues to serious problems.

The family decided to have her meet a psychiatrist to see what
could be done about her weeping. The psychiatrist who came to
see her was an elderly man who assured her she was all right. She
continued to weep. The psychiatrist experimented with medicat-
ing her. The medication was supposed to solve the problem but it
did not. The family brought in another psychiatrist who, when he
could not stop her weeping, recommended psychiatric hospital-
ization. The parents did not believe she should be hospitalized for
fear it would disrupt her entire life. The psychiatrist decided there
was something hidden in the woman's mind from her childhood
and that it should be brought out of her unconscious. Changes in
medication neither prevented her from weeping nor helped her understand the cause. She only wept. This psychiatrist became frus-
trated in the few weeks he was working with her; although she

improved, she continued to weep. He consulted another doctor because he wanted a therapist who was skilled in hypnosis. She was resistant to hypnosis and told her husband on the way to the hospital, "Nobody is going to hypnotize me."

Up to this point, the family and therapists have done everything wrong; Wendy was put through all the wrong situations. The following is a summary of what to do.

Puzzled by this weeping symptom of Wendy, the hypnotist knew that something more than conversation was needed. He did help her relax and feel more positive with each positive suggestion given. She wept but she was more cheerful. The therapist decided he would encourage the couple to come in for an interview together rather than one at a time as they had been doing. When they came in, the therapist asked the two of them if they planned ultimately to move back into their own house. The husband replied, "We'd like to move back in if we could but probably she won't. We'll wait until she is better." Wendy replied, "I'll never get better." And she wept. The therapist asked, "How is it to live with the in-laws?" Wendy said, "It isn't pleasant and I'm getting isolated in the family. When my husband comes home from work he goes to his mother to get a report on the baby, not to me. So my mother-in-law is taking over the baby."

Offer a Double Bind

"Do you ultimately plan to move back into your own house?" the therapist asked. Wendy replied, "Someday we'll move back into our own house." "It looks to me like you're more capable of being a mother than you realize," the therapist said. "Are you agreed that someday you are going to move back into your own house? Let's see. This is Monday. I think you can move back into your house this Thursday." Wendy was shocked. She said, "That's impossible. The place is dirty and needs cleaning. The baby's room needs painting." The therapist asked the husband what he thought about it. The husband said casually, "We could move back home today and get away from my family. My wife is taking care of the baby properly and she can do it." Wendy said, "That's impossible, I couldn't possibly move in, certainly not before Friday." The therapist, ignoring Wendy, asked the husband, "Would you agree to take off work to help her get the house organized and move by Friday?" The husband said, "I could stay home because I work for my father and could get a couple of weeks off and I also know how to take care of the baby." "You do not," Wendy replied. "I do too. I can do everything but nurse her," he insisted. Wendy stopped weeping. She was angry. Wendy shouted, "We couldn't possibly move into our house before Friday. Thursday is ridiculous." They began to talk about what was to be done to prepare the house for the baby. They were accepting the idea that someday they would have to go back to their house and it was just a matter of when. They finally agreed on Friday. Wendy was pleased to have chosen the day she wanted. After all the objections they had from his family, when they saw his parents, they announced to them that they were going to move back home on Friday. The grandparents looked baffled at this sudden action that was moving them into their own home Friday but they had enough of Wendy and were actually pleased that they were moving. On Thursday, the couple was so occupied getting the house in order that they didn't have time to remind Wendy to be helpless.

During that first week at home, Wendy called the therapist and asked to see him. She asked the therapist if he would come and visit her because she was worried about taking care of the baby and she continued to weep, although less often. The therapist asked, "How is the baby?" She said, "The baby is surprisingly cheerful, but I don't know why she should be." "I can come for lunch tomorrow," the therapist said. Wendy replied, "I don't know if I could take care of the baby and invite you, too." The therapist answered, "I expect a good lunch if I come because I always have good lunches." This directive seemed to get her focused on making a good lunch rather than on her competence as a mother. When the therapist visited, Wendy stopped her crying and served him a good lunch. Wendy talked while the baby sat smiling on her lap, obviously enjoying her. She told the therapist that she was thinking over her situation and why she has been weeping. She said, "I feel anxious because I cannot depend on my husband to be responsible." Her husband managed not to do what she needed. Her in-laws were difficult for her to deal with. Her friends weren't visiting because they didn't want to disturb her.

One case can illustrate a wide range of issues surrounding birth. A new baby can be a joyful event or bring difficulties. All sorts of relatives who may have been excluded become grandparents, aunts, uncles, stepparents, godparents, and cousins. Often a mother can become depressed and feel helpless. Fathers feel put upon by new responsibilities. "Becoming parents gave us too much responsibility," said Wendy. "It did not matter when we were just a couple, but it matters when we have a serious responsibility with a baby."

The husband did not like responsibility. He was a car salesman and not a very successful one. He liked going back home to his parents because of his wife's weeping, even though his wife didn't like being there. Giving the husband something to do is similar to prescribing rituals surrounding pregnancy and birth in the couvade* rituals practiced in many primitive societies. Staying home for two weeks to help his wife with the baby would show his commitment to his new family, something she perhaps doubted. You must always consider other people when resolving a problem. The in-laws wished to be helpful by taking them in. Then they had difficulty with the daughter-in-law and with each other. Mother-in-law took a position against the daughter-in-law and magnified

---

*Couvade is a French word that means to brood or hatch. It is a custom reported in many societies, including our own, in which the father develops symptoms or observes rituals surrounding pregnancy.

her difficulties because she was being helpless and weeping. The husband was not being helpful. What ultimately helped was getting Wendy organized.

> **The long-term goal of treatment should be the immediate goal.**

Within two weeks of moving into a place of their own, Wendy had her house in order, was having her friends over, and had stopped weeping. As she changed, the in-laws began to enjoy the baby and support her rather than criticize her. She had the freedom to invite them over when it was convenient for her. The couple made the proper transition from birth to the next stage of child rearing. Sammy began to be proud of his daughter.

> **The goal cannot be achieved as long as the living situation is inappropriate; the solution is to bring about a more normal context of living.**

In order to get back to a normal living situation as soon as possible after the birth of a child, the following suggestions are offered:

- Stress the problem of learning how to organize the couple's life, rather than the medical diagnosis.
- Arrange for mother to take care of the baby and hire someone to help if necessary.
- Treat the mother as capable.
- Include the husband in her program of improvement—to take responsibility for the care of the baby with specific tasks to do.

- Have her friends over to see the new baby. Arrange activities such as decorating their home or making lunch, that occupy her in some positive work.
- Assign tasks to in-laws when ready.

This case illustrates sharply that treatment can go surprisingly quickly if one adopts Erickson's premise that the long-term goal of treatment should be the immediate goal. If the ultimate "cure" is defined as the woman taking care of her own child in her own house with a husband willing to take responsibility, then the treatment should proceed immediately to achieve that end. The goal cannot be achieved as long as the living situation is inappropriate; the solution is to bring about a more normal context of living.

Chapter 3

Raising Kids

Parents have complex choices as they raise their children. There is major disagreement in the field regarding how to handle problems with children. One question is whether to involve the family or deal with the child individually. Another question is whether to interpret a child's extreme misbehavior as the result of parental conflicts. Still another issue is whether parents should use their own instincts and rely on information they have been exposed to over the years to parent, or whether they need to be taught how to parent. The directive approach involves the family and not just an individual child. It accepts the idea that parents have good instincts on how to parent and do not need to be trained. The therapist's task is not to teach parenting but to discuss the child's relationship to the family members and other people. Unlike therapies in which clients are required to interpret *why something is happening* in order to understand one another, the directive approach is primarily concerned with action. When kids make the family miserable, there are steps the family can take.

Children Who Fall Out

Every hour of every day presented a crisis in this family. The problem could be heard two blocks away because Sammy, the three-year-old, yelled whenever his family took him outside the house. He also yelled inside the house if he was told to do some-

Directive Family Therapy
Published by The Haworth Press, Inc., 2007. All rights reserved.
doi:10.1300/5883_04

39

thing or not to do something. Often he threw himself on the floor and banged on it with his fists while yelling. Seeming to imitate this erupting volcano, his two-year-old sister also regularly threw herself on the floor and screamed. These children might have stepped out of the nightmares of a couple who feared having children. Sammy appeared to be almost unmanageable unless physically restrained. He was also well known for his tantrums in his neighborhood and at the clinics and hospitals that his mother visited. Professionals were always advising her what to do about his yelling, but the advice had not proven helpful. The mother was asked what she thought the problem was. She responded, "After the baby came, [Sammy] didn't want to sit on the potty anymore. I tried to get him away from the bottle, but he still wanted to take the bottle." To get him to stop, she would say "Stop" or spank him.

In this family, the father and mother disagreed about whether there was a problem at all. The father said his son didn't have a problem, "he just has a habit of yelling and screaming and hollering." When the mother said there was something wrong with the boy, the father responded as if he himself had something wrong with him.

The approach taken with this family was to try to solve the problem without teaching the mother or father how to deal with children. Because both parents felt incompetent, this approach offered a chance to test the theory of whether parents really need to be taught how to raise their children. The focus would be on changing the sequences in the family using specific directives, including ordeals. In the interview, the mother was directed not to complain to the father when he came home from work, but to tell him when he asked that she handled everything okay. She was told that she was a competent person who would make the correct decisions when free to do so: "I think your instincts are fine and you can rely on them. What you'll be doing will be the right thing to do." Mother, however, continued feeling that Father was better at dealing with the children than she was. A paradoxical directive was given to change this. The therapist set up the situation by saying to the father, "The next time your son acts up, could you supervise your wife to get him to do whatever he should do? When he does something wrong again, you help her step-by-step to get him to do what she wants him to do." Such an ordeal forced her to rebel in the direction of more competence to demonstrate to the therapist that she was capable. As she showed that competence to the children, they responded by behaving better, and even became willing to separate from her by staying in the waiting room with the toys while she was in the interview room.

Besides helping the mother to be competent, the therapist helped her with her "nervous condition" with another paradoxical directive: "You need to take at least ten to fifteen minutes a day, and set it aside to be nervous and to be depressed. Get it all out of your way." The mother was helped to choose a time that seemed to be convenient—eight o'clock in the evening, just after the children were put to bed. However, on days when the children didn't misbehave and she enjoyed them, she didn't have to go through this depressed period. In this way, the mother was encouraged toward more good cheer and competence with the children but without any instruction in how to do that.

The couple was having trouble with their marriage. Mother said she never goes anywhere and feels neglected. The parents were asked to express affection for each other so the children would learn more about how to show affection. After considerable persuasion by the therapist, the couple agreed to show affection for each other regularly each day.

The parents remained together and the mother went to work. The children did what the parents asked without temper tantrums, and they were able to be apart from the parents and accepting of care from other people. The boy successfully attended nursery school, and later the daughter did also. The parents became more affectionate with each other.

This is a case example of extreme temper tantrums that were apparently caused by parental conflicts. The strategy used was to respect the instincts and impulses of the parents to do the right thing. Parents know, but don't know that they know. They did not require child-rearing education, which is a popular form of child therapy. Paradoxical directives were used. The mother, who was anxious and depressed, was told to set aside fifteen minutes a day to be depressed. In other words, you program the behavior that is causing you the trouble.

**Respect the instincts and impulses
of the parents to do the right thing.**

The mother also accepted the father's advice on how to make the children do what she wanted them to. When she acted more competently as a result, the children behaved. The message in this case is that parents are competent. The solution wasn't education, it was their willingness to take action.

Program the behavior that is causing you the trouble.

Bed Wetters

As children grow older, there are behaviors they must leave behind. Bed-wetting is an example of a physiological process where children have not yet learned control. Sometimes it is best to leave the parents out of the situation and allow bed wetters to cure themselves through directives. Other times the parents must give the task to the child. Here are a few examples by Dr. Milton Erickson from my conversations with him, on various ways he dealt with this problem. An important decision must be made as to whether the child is biologically mature enough to control his or her sphincter muscles, which may not yet be sufficiently developed to control bed-wetting. It can be a crisis for a family when the parents don't agree on the course of action.

Tell the Child to Do in a Special Way
What He or She Is Already Doing

I can think of a bed-wetting case where I told the parents, "Absolutely don't you dare go in your son's room. Don't you make the bed. Don't you change the linen. Don't do anything. Don't say anything. I'm handling it." So the parents really kept out of it completely in that sort of a fashion. Sometimes in the bed-wetting, you tell the child, "Now listen, you can't disappoint your parents all the time. They know darn well that you are going to wet the bed. That is what they honestly believe and nothing is going to change their minds. They're going say that to you over and over and over again. Now listen, it isn't a pleasing thing to ask of you, but it's a necessary thing. Now let's see, today is the third of December. I suppose, why not pick on December 13th. That'd be a good day. The thirteenth is considered an unlucky number. So on the night of the thirteenth, just go ahead and wet the bed. Even if you have to try pretty hard to do it, but wet it. Don't disappoint your parents. They know darn well you're going to do it, but you don't have to do it every night. So you pick the night you do it. As sure as he picks the night, he is saying, "I have control." But he doesn't know that. So he comes and tells you how hard it was to wet the bed deliberately. I told him, well it was worth it for your mother's sake. Now, the thirteenth, I suppose we can wait until the thirteenth of February, or January, or March, or June. You see that juggling back and forth, but you may have two deliberate bed-wettings, sometimes two or three, but you hold primarily in reserve that suggestion for February and January. You backed up June, March, you've gone way ahead, you've backed up. You're making progress. (Haley 1985b, pp. 127-132)

The child will sometimes put up a struggle when the parents are involved in treatment. Another approach is to have the child deal with the therapist and leave the parents out of it.

The other 12-year-old boy, regardless of what time his parents got him up, wet the bed at twelve o'clock. He would lie and rage at himself until about two o'clock. Then he'd get up, and simply walk to his parents' bedroom and insist on sleeping between them. Frequently they spanked him repeatedly but he went right back in between them for another spanking until they gave up. He didn't enjoy sleeping with them, they didn't enjoy it, and they all had broken sleep. I knew the boy wouldn't go on Boy Scouts hikes because he wet the bed. I knew his parents had bribed him with pet rabbits, and I knew his parents had given him a collection of minerals and stones and that he liked those, and that he had a Boy Scout blanket. So I raised the question of this self-punishment: that regardless of what his parents did, he wet the bed and he punished himself by lying in bed, and then, not satisfied with that punishment, he got up and went into his parents' bedroom for more punishment, and they gave it to him. Why didn't he take charge of his own punishments and deliberately and honestly and openly administer them to himself? We finally agreed that he should spread his stones out over the concrete floor, draping the Boy Scout blanket over them, go to bed, wet the bed at midnight, awaken, and instead of lying in a wet bed say, "Well, I want punishment and I'm going to administer it to myself," and get up and lie down on the blanket on the stones and sleep there the rest of the night. I am not absolutely certain of the length of time, but it was under a month that he gave up his rabbits because they were a bribe to him, kept his stones, and continued for approximately a month to sleep on the stones after midnight, until finally he decided that he'd had enough of that, he could sleep in his bed, the way he wanted to with a dry bed, and that was that. And I told him that if his mother found him sleeping on the stones, that he should tell her what he was doing was his own arrangement with the psychiatrist and that she could talk to me, but I wouldn't give her any satisfaction. I had in one of the parents. "You want me to take care of this boy? Let me do it in my own way. I'll send you a bill after the boy stops wetting his bed." (Haley, 1985b, pp. 127-132)

Prescribe the symptom but less often, and the child learns that he or she can have control.

There are so many conflicts between parents and a child with a problem. In these examples, Erickson has the parents stay out of the problem, but you can use Erickson's scripts with bed wetters:

1. Assign dates to perform the symptom so that the child learns that in order not to disappoint the parents he should perform the symptom on specified dates that are further and further apart. You are prescribing the symptom but less often, and the child learns that he can have control.
2. Have the child decide his own punishment if he wets the bed. This should be something that is an ordeal and more uncomfortable for the child than the symptom itself.
3. Another technique is not talking about bed-wetting, but using a metaphor or an example that can be equated to the symptom without mentioning the symptom directly. Have the child learn control.

Firesetters

Some problems are a routine part of growing up, but others can have severe consequences and must be handled with the seriousness they are due, because children can sometimes exhibit dangerous behavior. Children enter a stage when they discover hierarchy, testing out power as they grow up. Sometimes this takes the form of opposing their parents. Instead of being exasperated, parents can learn techniques to introduce play into the power struggle. One problem behavior seen among children that has potentially hazardous consequences is enthusiasm for setting fires. As an example, a family came to a clinic to solve an emergency problem. Their seven-year-old son was setting fires. In fact, he set fires while walking through the clinic by lighting matches and dropping them in the wastebaskets of the offices. The family was assigned to a young social worker who just graduated from school. She protested to her supervisor that she did not know how to cure a firesetter. The supervisor said there would be a staff meeting on her case in a week, so she would learn what could be done about the problem. The following week and several fires later, a staff session was held regarding the firesetting boy. The staff talked about the emotional causes of firesetting, but the young social worker learned nothing that would help her stop the firesetting. She was sitting in her office crying when a colleague walked by and saw her. He asked her, "Why the crying?" She explained that she didn't know what to do with this case she was assigned. The colleague was a behavior therapist and he said, "Let's see what we can do. To light fires, the boy has to light matches. You might give him a nickel for every match he can bring to the parents without it being lit." The social worker liked this directive since she needed something to do. The parents enjoyed having someone advise them with a serious problem. The boy liked the idea of getting nickels if he stopped lighting fires. The firesetting stopped. Everyone was pleased. You can reward clients for stopping the symptomatic behaviors they should not be doing.

Another solution is seen in one of the earliest family therapy cases on video by Braulio Montalvo. He saw a single mother with a little girl who set the mattress on fire when the mother was out working and the babysitter wasn't responsible. Mother was angry at her little girl for endangering the home and because she was Daddy's favorite and Daddy had left the mother. The therapist directed the mother to teach the girl to make safe fires and help her to be pleased that she was competent at building a safe fire. Rather than stressing how bad the child was, the solution stressed education.

Reward clients for stopping the symptomatic behaviors they should not be doing.

Another example involved a boy whose father was in the army. The son set a potentially very dangerous fire to an ammunition dump. The therapist convinced the boy that he had not learned to set a good fire, and directed the father to take his son to the library to learn to set fires correctly. The father had been neglecting the boy, and this directive provided a way for them to spend time together. When the boy quit setting fires, he and his father went on to do other things together like fishing. In the case of a potentially deadly symptom, a pleasant ordeal was assigned.

Miss Manners

A little girl's family had a variety of problems—sex abuse, physical abuse, and drug abuse—all centered around one little girl called Patti. She was upsetting the school and her mother by masturbating in class every day until she had rubbed herself raw. All the children in class stared at her, and the unsympathetic teacher sent her out in the hall. Mother said, "Ever since I can remember, she [has done] it; as young as 16 to 18 months, she did it in a cart in the supermarket. (The mother imitates a pelvic movement). I can always tell because her face blotches up." Father and Mother had broken up. Father physically abused both the mother and the daughter. Mother described what happened in one instance: "He squeezed Patti's cheeks until her mouth bled. When she was crying, he would slap her and shake her. When I protested, he beat the hell out of me." Mother suspected that he sexually abused the daughter, but there was no evidence. Mother was a nurse and provided drugs for her husband so he wouldn't beat her. The grandfather, whom they turned to for help, exposed himself and upset everyone. The mother could not take any time away from Patti and said, "My own mother can't handle her and she pushes my mother to the limit. I feel like I'm going to unravel."

Although the case was complex, the solution was simple. To comfort her, the mother had been routinely rocking Patti when she masturbated. The therapist told Patti that she had a plan: "For every day you don't masturbate in school, you get a reward from your mom. This is the kind of behavior I see from much younger children than you. What I would like to suggest is each evening you [to the mother] hold and rock Patti. [To Patti] You can spend 15 minutes to half an hour just rocking on the days you don't masturbate in school." Mother adds, talking to Patti, "I'm going to get a special rocking chair and everyday you haven't "cooched" or masturbated is the technical term, I'm going to rock you." The therapist added, "Sing her a nursery rhyme since this is a small child's behavior." When they came in the following week, Patti had masturbated once and the mother refused to rock her that day. Mother said, "The rocking has worked. The teacher called me and said I can't believe the change in her behavior." Patti stopped masturbating. The family then agreed to have the grandmother babysit one night a week while the mother had a night out with her friends.

Reward desired behavior, not undesired behavior.

Mother had been rocking Patti when she masturbated to comfort her. This caused Patti to masturbate to get rocked. The solution was to direct the mother to do the opposite— to rock her only when she did not masturbate. This approach eliminated the problem behavior. The mother comforted the daughter when she behaved, rather than rewarding her for misbehavior. Reward desired behavior, not undesired behavior.

Only on Sunday

A mother and son had been to therapists for five years and tried everything to solve the ten-year-old boy's embarrassing problem. The therapist* decided to talk to George alone. "Tell me," said the therapist, "Do you know of any place in your house where you can go and masturbate all by yourself?" The therapist was asking about private masturbation because George's problem was public masturbation without pleasure. He masturbated in front of his mother and sisters and at school, had been hospitalized once for blood in the urine, and wore holes in the crotch of his pants.

The therapist developed a trusting relationship with George, who agreed to follow his plan. The directive to the boy was to mark down on a chart every time he masturbated until the next interview. At the next interview, they carefully went over the chart to find out what day it felt best, which turned out to be Sunday. The second directive was to have him do it eight times next Sunday, because that was the only day he was enjoying it. "So you might have to get up a little earlier to start." By encouraging excessive masturbation on one day it would be possible to make it an ordeal. The next step was to punish the boy for masturbating on some other

---

*John Lester

day by having him do it more on Sunday. The therapist also focused on other activities the boy could participate in, such as basketball. Because George had not followed the agreement, the therapist punished him by instructing him to repeatedly unzip his pants, take them off, and fold them neatly at the end of the bed with the creases together. George repeated this routine again and again in front of the therapist until it became tedious. The ordeal was working and George masturbated only on Sunday. The therapy began to disengage Mother from Son and focus on his sister.

**Encouraging repetition of the symptomatic
behavior can make it an ordeal.**

The problem was solved in eight interviews over a period of ten weeks. In a five-year follow-up, the symptom was not resumed, although it was never never determined whether his private masturbation was pleasurable because it was so private.

Can Parents Be More Powerful Than Kids?

Parenting is a matter of power. Dr. Erickson has a useful example of parents gaining power when children fight by imposing an ordeal on the children. Son Number One and Son Number Two were learning to struggle for power in the family. This took the form of fighting, with the elder calling the younger one "Bad boy, bad boy," and the younger one screaming back, "No, I'm not; No, I'm not!" This exasperated Dr. Erickson and the whole family. Dr. Erickson told the boys that on a day which was convenient for him, he would teach them to behave. The day came when both boys had interesting things they wanted to do. Erickson put them in a room, closed the door, and told them to yell "Bad boy, bad boy" and "No, I'm not; No, I'm not!" just as they had all along. If they did it right, they could leave and do the things they wanted. When they seemed to lose enthusiasm, Dr. Erickson instructed them to yell louder. This activity went on for three hours. Subsequently, it was no longer necessary to deal with this issue. If the boys even thought of yelling at one another and disturbing the family, they stopped (Haley, 1985b).

This is an example of a paradoxical directive—leading the child to refrain from the undesirable behavior by having him do it in an exaggerated way on command.

Out of Control Kids

What seems a milder technique, called the Italian technique, can actually be more powerful because it threatens abandonment. With a problem daughter who was out of control, the parents were advised to take some action. One explanation for her unruliness was that she was afraid her parents would separate, and if she made trouble, they would stay together to deal with her. The parents had angry scenes with the daughter, who wouldn't do what they wanted.

The parents were directed to put a note on the kitchen table while the daughter was out of the house. The note read, "We have gone away." When the daughter came home, she saw the note and didn't know whether they had gone for the day or forever. The older daughter was left to take care of her, which she did anyway. The note was put out on Saturday and on Saturday night the parents were not there. On Sunday morning the parents were not there. On Sunday noon the parents were not there. On Sunday evening the parents had not arrived. When the house was empty of parents on Monday, the daughter was afraid they had gone away for good. When the parents did appear, the girl told them she was shocked by them leaving like that. She said, "I didn't think Dad would ever leave me like that." The mother said, "Parents have a right to go away if they choose when a child misbehaves." The daughter, afraid the parents would not put up with her and would leave her, began to behave and dealt with the parents with respect when threatened with abandonment. The daughter thought that the parents were having enough trouble with each other that they might separate, unless she provided a problem for them to deal with together.

A few days of vacation for exasperated parents allows children to learn how much they need their parents. In this example, an older sister remained in the house. One would not leave a child alone without supervision.

The Boy Who Wouldn't Go to School

Paul was a thirteen-year-old boy who, according to his parents, was so severely depressed that he cried continuously and could not go to school. They tried different tactics, including actually carrying the boy to school and leaving him at the teacher's door. He returned home, refusing to stay in school. They asked his pediatrician if the medication he was taking for allergies could cause this depression. It was concluded that it was not caused by medication. The father and mother were a middle-class couple with two other children, and were concerned about their son. The father said he did not understand the behavior and told Paul, "You have to get hold of yourself." In response, the boy became more depressed. Mother focused on being kind to their son and tried to quiet her husband. In desperation they hired a therapist to help. Mother reported that the therapist said, "Don't do anything at all to put pressure on the boy to go to school. Don't discuss school; just keep him calm and make no demands." Paul responded by not going to school and being depressed.

The Action That Made the Change

The lack of change in their son led the parents to seek the help of a psychiatrist. He took an opposite approach to this problem and told the parents that the boy had to go to school. This therapist did not focus on the cause of the depression, but only on the actions needed to solve the problem. The cause had been discussed by previous therapists. The parents accepted the idea reluctantly and told Paul he had to go to school the next morning.

The therapist instructed the parents while Paul sat with his head down. "We feel it is critically important to go school. Since Mother is an expert in the family, I want you to take him to school. Father should help load him in the car. Each one should hold his hand and walk him into the school. Mother is to sit in the classroom with him. Mother is to go to gym class with him. If he doesn't want to participate, Mother, you hold his hand so he can tolerate the anxiety." The idea was that a thirteen-year-old boy does not want his mother in class with him, particularly in gym. Crying, Paul yelled, "I'm not going to school with you there." The therapist replied, "That is something your parents will have to help you with." Even if the parents had been in disagreement before, at this interview they were persuaded to send Paul to school the next day. Mother said, "I will stay with you all day." Still crying, Paul said, "I'm not going." Normalizing the situation, the therapist said, "He is certainly not severely depressed. He is behaving like a rebellious thirteen-year-old." The interview ended with the boy crying and the parents agreeing to force him to go to school the next day.

**Do not focus on the cause of the symptom,
but on the actions needed to solve the problem.**

A short time later, the mother called the therapist. "I did a terrible thing. My son said he was going to run away and not go to school. I worried about him running away, so I told him he didn't have to go to school. What should I do now?" The therapist said, "You tell your son that sometimes mothers tell lies and I shouldn't have said you don't have to go to school because you do." The son went to school the next morning without the mother being in the room with him and that ended the problem.

When children are in a power struggle with their parents, in most cases the parents should win. It can be done. They should not be afraid of the consequences of standing their ground. If children will not go to school, the therapist should direct the parents to take them to school and sit with them, which they will not appreciate.

Fear of Dogs

One of the earliest family therapy interviews on video, if not the first, was with a family composed of a father, a mother, an eight-year-old boy, and a six-year-old girl. The presenting problem was that the boy, Leslie, had never in his life been able to associate with dogs. He was largely confined to his home because he avoided dogs on the street. He would even run from them directly into traffic. His parents were afraid to let him go outside alone. He went into therapy for a year with no improvement. During that time they bought him a dog and tried to desensitize him little by little but it did not help.

Encourage a symptom to help the client get over it.

The therapist in this case* first encouraged the father, who was a letter carrier, to explain to his son how he wards off dogs when they bark at him. The next step was to get a dog into the home. This was difficult because it had been tried before and failed. The therapist said, "All right, Leslie, so it sounds as though you have to learn a few things. I want you to go and adopt a puppy. But you pick one who is afraid. How would you know if he's afraid?" Leslie replied, "I would say a dog that would go away from you."

---

*Mariano Barrigan, MD

The therapist explained the plan clearly, with the parents agreeing. "I want you to adopt a puppy that you think is afraid, and I want you to cure the dog. With the help of your parents, you are all together to cure this dog." They went out and chose a dog and brought him to the session. The boy would not touch the dog. The therapist told him to do something to get this little puppy over his fears. The father said, "Pick up the dog." Leslie replied, "I can't pick him up." The parents mentioned that he already had held the dog, although he would not do it in the session. The parents agreed that the boy was improving in the first session. They talked about their own conflicts so the focus was not always on the dog. After Leslie had been playing with the dog, the therapist asked him to "trick the little puppy into thinking that you are afraid of him." Les answered, "Run from him?" The therapist said, "Yes; act scared." The parents were puzzled by the paradoxical technique of encouraging a symptom to get over it.

The parents had not been getting along and needing to help their son brought them together. The therapy enabled the parents to get along better. Les did fine with dogs and came with his own dog to the sessions.

In cases of crippling fear and panic, therapists need to come up with creative approaches to help clients overcome their anxiety. In this case, the phobic boy was asked to find a puppy, something that needed him and was afraid, and teach the puppy to be unafraid by playing with it in the room with the parents. The action was a metaphor for him to get over his own fears.

VIOLENCE IN SCHOOL

Parents want their children to be socially polite, respectful, assertive, and caring. The most serious problems occur when violence is threatened or carried out.

The Eight-Year Old Who Broke His Teacher's Nose

Art was an eight-year-old boy who broke his teacher's nose and gave her a concussion that put her in the hospital overnight. It was hard to imagine this little freckle-faced boy throwing temper tantrums, tearing up the house, and getting into other serious trouble in school. He was taken to the principal's office and his mother and father were called. They persuaded the school that Art wouldn't harm anyone ever again. He was a likeable boy so he managed not to be expelled. But his behavior was severe enough that the parents took "parents' effectiveness training," which did not help.

The solution to stop the violence was simple—an old behaviorist tradition that required action—but following through was complicated. The therapist* was an expert with children. She sent the other siblings out so the father, the mother, and Art could deal with the problem without being distracted. We assumed that this was a hierarchical problem in which the parents felt helpless in the face of their son's extreme behavior and needed to be empowered to take charge of the situation. First, the boy was encouraged to describe just what happened at school. This involved acting out what happened in front of the parents, including getting the janitor to protect the teacher. He had hit the teacher and denied that this behavior was a serious problem. The therapist saw the parents alone and told them they had to stop this violence because their son was too casual about it and would end up in real trouble. The mother and father talked at some length about how impossible it was to control the boy. The therapist convinced them it was necessary and could be quite simple. We advised the parents to employ the technique that many families use: If he had a temper tantrum, they were to put him in his room for half an hour. Despite many objections from the parents, who expected resistance from their son, they agreed that they would put him in his room if he made any

---

*Marcha Ortiz

trouble. The father was doubtful he could stop the boy from acting in a violent manner. The therapist asked the mother to bring the boy in from the waiting room and directed the parents to tell him that he would be put in his room if he were violent or angry. Art said he could break the door down. His father said that they would put on a stronger door. Art said he would break it down even if it were a metal door. During the week the boy was angry, started swearing, and broke something in the house. The mother said, "I will put you in your room." The father was not there at the time. The mother did succeed in holding the door until the father got home and helped her. The solution was simple. The problem was defined clearly. The parents pulled together to do the task. If you are violent you get put in your room by yourself. They talked about what was violent and what wasn't and made it clear.

Empower parents to take charge of the situation.

They came in the next week and there had been no problems. In the follow-up several months later, Art had not harmed nor threatened anyone. The school appreciated that. The therapist asked the parents what they thought had made the therapy successful. "I was really surprised to get a solution," said the father. "I've never had dealings with professional people, but I thought it was all deeply theoretical and it was going to take a year to pull an answer out of the air, and a team of analysts. And then your solution of putting Art in his room and putting a latch on the door really surprised me. But we tried it in good faith, and it worked so well I couldn't believe it. It kind of restored my faith in being firm." The mother said, "There was a tremendous amount of resentment. I was really puzzled by the solution, but willing to try it. I thought, why should he have a tantrum and ruin the whole family for the rest of the day? He should just be separated."

Encourage parents to reach an agreement about how to handle the problem.

In summary, the therapist gathered information about the violence by having the child reenact what happened. The parents were encouraged to reach an agreement about how to handle the problem. Parents must agree to restrain children if they are violent or bad-tempered. Adults should be encouraged to resolve their own conflicts. Even though it may not be apparent, the misbehavior of a child often reflects conflicts between family members.

Another example of children taking charge is when they have a severe illness. They may become very demanding and often the parents cannot refuse them anything because they feel so sorry for them and so guilty. Parents in such difficult situations must be firm for the child's welfare.

The Boy Who Can't Stop Fighting

Sam was a nine-year-old boy who was obsessed with fighting. He dreamed about it and could not help it. He was put in one school after another with children just like him. He had seen all his male relatives die by the age of twenty-five.

Sam, his mother, and two brothers came for therapy. Since nothing they tried had worked before, the mother was directed to be in charge of having the fighting boy teach his good brother to fight, since he should not carry all the burden of misbehaving.

> THERAPIST: Some kids can take turns at being bad. What would happen if you trade places with your brother and he can have a bad week next week?
>
> SAM: He doesn't know how to be bad.
>
> THERAPIST: You have to teach him.

This paradox is encouraging the behavior you are trying to eliminate. Nobody in the room was talking much until this playing suggestion broke the ice. The kids understood this as play and not combat and practiced it in the therapy room. They were willing to play—playing in the sense of a metaphor.

One of the studies of Gregory Bateson showed that animals must differentiate between the bite of combat and the bite of play and every once in a while they don't differentiate and they bite each other and get into a battle. Bateson was interested in the fact that you must be able to communicate on two levels in order to play—communicate about communication. Children learn how to establish a relationship and then begin to play within the relationship (Haley, 1955). But often you can have kids pass the symptom from one to another and what it does is thin it out.

In a seemingly impossible situation with more than one child involved, you can direct the problem child to teach the good child the bad behavior in order to have some new skills. This makes the problem a game of play rather than combat. If you can encourage a symptom in a different context, you can do away with it. By putting an adult in charge of this game, the proper hierarchy of adults in charge is reinforced. Alternately, a child's aggressive behavior can be channeled into something positive, such as learning martial arts.

If you can encourage a symptom in a different context, you can do away with it.

The boys were obsessed with watching wrestling on TV. Since the stepfather would not come to the sessions, empowering him involved getting him to participate in activities with the boys. This special treatment of him could shift his low position in the family hierarchy. He was encouraged to take the boys to a wrestling match, which brought them closer together. Not many professionals would have encouraged involvement in wrestling, but it made the stepfather special in the eyes of the boys so they would respect him. Integrating a peripheral stepfather is one of the techniques of family therapy dating from the 1950s. A stepfather should be included in the family even though he is not the biological father. Often there is uncertainty as to how much authority he has. He should be encouraged to participate in family discussions and actions. If the stepfather is marginalized in any way, encouraging positive involvement with his stepchildren can improve his relationship with them. In this case, the boys began to get along better with their stepfather. The fighting obsession subsided and the fighting stopped.

The Overprotected Son

The therapist* was recruited from the local community and trained by Haley, Minuchin, and Montalvo. Haley supervised the case. A mother brought her twelve-year-old son in. She was very overprotective. She took him to school, and volunteered at the playground. She took him home and did not let the boy out of the house. There was a possibility that the boy was learning disabled, but it was difficult to determine because he was so protected. The father had died.

> **Respond matter-of-factly to clients'
> experiences to normalize the situation.**

The therapist interviewed the mother without ever suggesting she had been overprotective. He persuaded her that the boy was getting to an age where he should be okay on the streets. He persuaded her to allow the boy to play on the streets while she sat on

*Pete Urquart

the front porch and still watched him. She did this during the week. The next week the therapist suggested that the boy go to the corner and return safely. By the third week, the boy was going to the school yard and playing basketball. During the three weeks, the therapist talked to the mother about a variety of things. The mother revealed that the boy had told her that he had talked to the father. Instead of taking a diagnostic posture, the therapist asked what the father had said to him. The boy said that his father told him he should have a bicycle. The therapist asked the mother about the bicycle. She said that he could have one but he couldn't ride it. In time, she allowed him to ride it. The mother also reported that sometimes at night the deceased father would come up the stairs, lie down next to her and sigh, and then go downstairs. The therapist told her that sometimes a mother misses a husband so much that she hears him and sees him, and that this would most likely go away in time.

Some therapists might tell the mother that she was overprotective and make her feel guilty. This approach could lead the boy to do something reckless, which would then give her an excuse to be overprotective. Some therapists might also say that the appearance of the father was a hallucination and therefore the boy was having a psychotic experience. The mother revealed her own experience only after the therapist responded so matter-of-factly to the boy's hallucination. This therapist was easy to supervise because he was very practical.

Paying Children to Get Rid of Symptoms

One complicated physical abuse case involved seven professionals dealing with a mother, a ten-year-old son, and eight-year-old twin girls. The father of the twins lost his temper and beat his ten-year-old stepson to the point that he had to be hospitalized. The father went to jail on a criminal child abuse charge. The children were removed from the home and placed in foster homes.

Therapy began when they were back with the mother. The present-ing problem was constant fighting among them and the mother was thinking of giving them up again, which would have been tragic after so much effort to get them back with her. The goal was to clarify a hierarchy in the family, with the mother in charge of the boy, who would be in charge of the twins. The plan was to pay the children for not hitting. The family needed to agree that if they were violent, nobody would get the money. The therapist* would motivate the children by paying them 50 cents for not hitting. The mother would decide if any hitting had occurred, which estab-lished the hierarchy of her in charge.

**Paradox with children can be effective
in stopping symptoms.**

The therapist defined a hit as follows: "So, in this family a hit would mean body contact, head, body, foot, and also an intention to hit. What if some hitting went on and you weren't in the room, Mom, and somebody comes and says, Mom, Mom, they hit me, but you didn't see it; would that count?"

"No" replied the twins. "So Mom has to see the hit?" asked the therapist. The twins answered "Yes," and the therapist continued, "No hitting. No ifs, ands, or buts. There is no hitting. No hitting in this family." "Period," echoed the twins. "If you hit, you don't get the 50 cents. You lose the game," added the therapist. The twins wanted to know "Who gives the 50 cents?" and the therapist an-swered, "I'm giving it to Mom and Mom will give it to you next week" (Haley & Richeport-Haley, 2003, pp. 82-83).

At the next interview, the family indicated that there had been one hit, but it was decided that the 50 cents would be given for ef-

---

*Mary Ferguror, PsyD

fort. Giving the money for good behavior was like giving an allowance.

A second strategy used in this case was to propose a paradox to solve the misbehavior and to reinforce a proper family hierarchy. The therapist referred to one twin as the evil twin and the other as the good twin. "A possibility would be to say that the evil twin has had this burden too long—being evil. And it's the other twin's turn to have it sometimes." (J. H.)

In a playful manner with props the therapist directed the twins to take turns being evil. The brother coached and the mother supervised the argument. This is a paradoxical approach because the therapist was instructing the evil twin to be evil and the good twin to be good. The evil twin was behaving good when she behaved badly on instruction. Paradox with children can be effective in stopping symptoms.

**In court-ordered cases, one therapist
must take charge of the case.**

The family therapist took control of the case and with permission from three court-appointed therapists was able to bring the father jailed for beating the stepson into one therapy session. He apologized to the family and embraced the stepson and other members of the family in a very moving interview. The goal in cases of violence is to ensure that no harm comes to anyone again. In a one-year follow-up, the therapy was a success.

Chapter 4

Young People

Being an adolescent is confusing. One can hear a fourteen-year-old saying, "I can decide my own life, thank you." This mind-set often leads to a debate between parent and child and inevitably a power struggle. Parents face a new batch of problems when their previously accepted authority is questioned by a child who is becoming more independent. Families are unsure what is normal. I recall friends who had a daughter and their family seemed very amiable, so much so that a researcher studying types of families wanted to classify them as a normal family. When the time came to test the family, the mother refused to be interviewed. She said, "We don't have a normal family. Our daughter is registering for college and the whole family is upset." This anecdote illustrates the idea that families can be viewed not as being of one type or another, but as having different reactions to the stages of the life cycle. Another consideration is ethnicity. Often the child and the parents were born in different countries. For example, an Italian family had a mother and a fifteen-year-old daughter who argued at length because the daughter wanted to date like the other American girls in school did. The mother debated the daughter at length on this issue, with the daughter saying "Everyone dates at fifteen in America," and the mother opposing this practice. The mother sought to support her position by taking her daughter to visit her own mother in Italy. She told her mother the circumstances. Instead of supporting her, the grandmother said "I think it's wonder-

Directive Family Therapy
Published by The Haworth Press, Inc., 2007. All rights reserved.
doi:10.1300/5883_05

ful that fifteen-year-olds can date. We never could date when I was young." Angry, the mother took her daughter back to America and gave in on the dating issue. Both young people and parents can have trouble adapting to changing times.

Adolescence is one of the most ambiguous stages of the family life cycle. The parents' goal is to teach the child to function successfully outside the home and to be self-supporting in the long run. This means having friendships outside the family that are supportive and positive. The process of separation starts at birth and intensifies during the teen years, when problems often develop. The child is having new experiences and so are the parents, who may be threatened by the prospect of the child's growing independence. Young people can gain power by threatening to leave; the parents fear it might really happen and so they give in on an argument. In many cases, the parents have a troubled marriage at the point where their daughter or son is entering adolescence. If the problems lead to divorce, as they often do, the family has to reconstitute itself in separate households.

Families can be affected by a variety of outside forces, such as economic crises, lost jobs, wars, or a spouse becoming involved with someone else. In new families, stepchildren and stepparents must be smoothly integrated into the existing family. Sometimes separated or divorced parents use the children in struggles with each other. Children and adolescents often believe it is their job to hold the parents together. This can be done either calmly or by making so much trouble that the parents have to stay together to deal with a young person. Children of any age can and do function as stabilizing forces in the family by keeping them together in times of difficulty.

A Teenager Rebels Against the Family

Peggy's parents had called the police because of all of the things she did when she did not get her own way. She threatened to cut herself with razor blades. She got out of a moving car on the highway. She wouldn't go to school. She reported her father for abuse, which was not true. She fought in school and threatened her older brother. She said her boyfriend was more important than her parents. The family did not do anything that the previous therapist had told them to do. They were so distressed they wanted to place her outside the home. The issue was the struggle for power in the family hierarchy. When the family came to the session, Peggy was clearly winning the power struggle. She said she liked to have her own way whether the parents liked it or not. The issue when they arrived at the interview with the therapist was her insistence that she should be driven to see her boyfriend, who was not that far away. The parents liked the boyfriend but did not want her to see him whenever she wanted to. The therapist did an exploration interview to clarify the problems. He listened to Peggy in a matter-of-fact way and asked her what she was doing to stay out of juvenile detention. She said she didn't like anyone to say "no" to her.

The therapist* was an expert with adolescents. He led Peggy into a discussion of what the rules should be in relation to the boyfriend. Peggy established her own rules of when she would see her boyfriend and how she was to behave with the family. She wrote down on a piece of paper the days she would see him: Monday, Thursday, and Saturday. Her parents agreed to drive her on those days. Similar tactics had been tried before and failed.

On the day of the interview, the parents were going to be near the boyfriend's place of employment, but it was not one of the days on the list that Peggy made. She began to rage that she wanted to go with them that very day so that she could see the boyfriend. For the first time, the parents said they would not take her because it was not one of the days that she had agreed upon. Peggy tore up the rules and insisted she would go if she wanted. The fa-

---

*Neil Schiff, PhD

ther and mother pulled together. The therapist told Peggy that tearing up the rules was unacceptable because she had made them up herself.

The Gandhi technique involves the whole family staying at home with the problem person at the risk of losing jobs or time at school.

The therapist proposed another directive. If Peggy was misbehaving in any way, the whole family would have to stay home from work or school for twenty-four hours. This directive is known as the Gandhi technique, and involves the whole family staying at home with the problem person at the risk of losing jobs or time at school. Peggy responded to this by yelling and complaining. She apparently saw that life would be difficult if they were all at home together.

The next session revealed that Peggy had behaved herself and the parents had enforced the rules. She stopped being childish and was a young lady. Her teachers said she had improved remarkably. The parents had been planning to renew their vows and did so in three months. Apparently they resolved marital issues when the parenting issues were solved.

The primary action was the threat that she would have to stay home with her family for twenty-four hours if she misbehaved. Most families cannot endure that much closeness. The therapist was skillful at this approach. For the first time, the parents presented a unified front to their daughter, who knew they would enforce the rules in the home. Having the daughter write her own rules for her parents to enforce with severe consequences made her more apt to follow them.

Mother-Daughter Incest

Sandy's lawyer referred her to family therapy after she turned herself in to the police after sexually molesting her stepniece, Joy, for six months. She came in with her three children, a daughter age eight, and two sons, ages seven and eight. In reaction to the abuse, the thirteen-year-old stepniece was taken out of the home and placed in foster care. She was not present. The therapist was a minister. He and Haley decided as a goal before the session to have them be a normal family. Sandy described her separation three-and-a-half years ago from her husband, who had been molesting the stepniece who had come to live with them when she was five. Joy and Sandy never hit it off and Sandy resented having the young girl around. When the husband left the home, social workers tried to get Sandy to be more affectionate with Joy. The therapist got the sexual details from Sandy. "It just so happened that one day when we were hugging, I got sexually aroused. I liked the idea of being close and having someone caring for me. I don't consider myself gay. To me I wasn't abusing her. I didn't force her. I got sexually aroused by the affection." Their sexual relationship grew to several times a week, sometimes with Joy initiating the affection. The therapeutic goal was to get them back together as a family. Even if that were not possible, the therapist should give them hope that someday they will get back together again. The three children were brought in and said that they missed their big sister.

The mother was arrested and placed in a prerelease center for one year. Haley and the therapist visited her. Joy was placed in a foster home. She ran away several times and tried to call her mother on the phone but Sandy would not speak to her. The other children were placed with the grandmother. Child Protective Services refused to allow the mother and Joy to ever be in the same room again. The therapist asked the foster mother to come to therapy with Joy so she could see Sandy. She refused. Sandy blossomed and got a job. She was permitted to come to therapy sessions with her other children. She was then able to return home and take care of her younger children. Sometime later the social workers were persuaded to allow Sandy and Joy to come to a therapy session if they provided Joy with an individual therapist. Joy was undecided whether she wanted to live with the mother or her grandmother.

> **The family approach allows that the family can change, which contrasts with the courts, which want contact to cease between the perpetrator and the abused.**

Most of the time in this case was spent dealing with authorities and colleagues and only a small portion in therapy sessions. The directive was to the mother to improve herself, which she did. The family approach allows that the family can change, which contrasts with the courts, which want contact to cease between the perpetrator and the abused. Both sides have legitimate although conflicting positions.

PROBLEMS WITH DRUGS

The Dope Girl

Seventeen-year-old Lucille stole sixteen thousand dollars from her mother's bank account. She made her theft more evident by doing it at the ATM machine, which took her picture. She was an addict who had taken every variety of drugs and sold drugs in high school. Her parents brought her to a therapist,* who held a meeting with the parents and Lucille. The therapist saw Lucille alone

---

*Neil Schiff, PhD

first for an interview. Both parents had declined to have her live with them. She said she couldn't go to either parent to live and something had to be done with her that night. The parents were looking for a place for her to stay. When the therapist asked what she preferred, she replied, "All drugs, just anything, pot, hash, opium, LSD, mushrooms, cocaine, nitrous oxide, PCP, and ecstasy." Her father and mother, a middle-class suburban family, were divorced and both were remarried. The mother's second marriage ended in divorce. The therapist asked Lucille, "Did your mother and father think you looked bad?" Lucille replied, "Yeah, I looked really bad. I used a lot of Visine. I rarely came home. My mom didn't really want to believe it." When Lucille stole money, it gave some power to the mother to press charges if she took drugs. Lucille did not want to go to prison or a rehab center, and the mother threatened her with that. Lucille said, "I was going to a drug-free school, Aftercare, AA and NA meetings. It gets on your nerves after awhile. This is why I relapsed. Gee, it was boring. Maybe I can wake up the next day and do the same thing. Everything is more fun when you're on drugs. I did everything high. I saw a shrink when I was five. I had been in two rehabs, two outpatient treatments, five shrinks, two family therapists. When is it enough? I know all the information." At the end she said partly jokingly that she would give up drugs if she didn't have to go to therapy ever again. Lucille continued, "You live once. Why not have a good time? That's why I don't want to spend my life in an institution. F*** that!"

The parents had been inadequate in dealing with her and could not agree with each other as parents. Lucille wanted to be turned loose without any supervision and the mother wanted her never to touch drugs again. Father wanted to ignore her and appeared at the family session as a dutiful father. The mother had not been very astute regarding what was happening when Lucille was living with her. Lucille would have as many as sixty phone calls a day arranging to sell drugs from their home.

The family had decided to place Lucille in a halfway house. They took her to the facility that evening, where drugs were forbidden. The next morning she was found smoking marijuana and was kicked out of the halfway house. Mother had said that she would have her arrested if she had any more drugs, so with this relapse she followed through with her threat to jail her. She brought her to the police station. The police said the matter could be handled outside of jail if she would be a police informer on the kids in high school. The mother became so angry that the police wanted to make her daughter an informer on her friends, she withdrew the charges and took her back in her home that night. The mother went into therapy with the family therapist the next day. The mother became angry in the interview and shouted at her daughter, which she had not done before. She said to Lucille, "There are two simple things you have to do to keep these charges off your back. Stay clean and don't steal any money. You've stolen $16,000. Isn't that enough? You've put every drug into your body known to man. You did these things to me as well as to yourself. It stopped being just you when you stole it from me. Or I will use everything in my power to see you don't do it anymore." The mother had changed from simply being unwilling to accept her daughter's addiction to being willing to press charges to send her daughter to jail, because she would have to leave the juvenile hall at eighteen years of age and be treated as an adult. This change in the mother's attitude made a difference in the case.

Mother arranged to have the daughter pay back her debt. The daughter would not come to therapy and behaved as if she were not taking drugs and got a job as a receptionist. She also got her GED. Mother was getting her own life straightened out in the therapy, which took the burden off the daughter. In a follow-up, Lucille had started college and had a boyfriend. She was not taking drugs as far as was known. The turning point was when the parents took responsibility and agreed on the severe consequence of a long jail sentence if the daughter took drugs again.

Mother and Father and Stepmother presented a united front to Lucille that if she did not stop taking drugs they would demand severe consequences and have her arrested. They insisted also that she pay back the debt she owed. The firmness worked. It gave them the power to stop the daughter from taking drugs.

Families often don't know that they can intervene and do something about the drug problems of relatives.

When a young person becomes addicted to drugs, the parents have a decision to make. They can use the forces in the family to end the addiction, or they can hand the problem to experts, who will put the young person in a group with addicts in court-ordered treatment. When the family can resolve the problem, they will benefit as well as the addict. Families often don't know that they can intervene and do something about the drug problems of relatives.

A Young Man Was Hooked on Marijuana

Edwin was arrested several times for drug possession and dealing. The last time he had been threatened by the court with a serious sentence that could put him in jail for years. In the family was a grandmother, an older brother named Papo, and several other adult siblings. Since the family had previously lost a father, Papo tended to take care of the family as a father would. The young woman therapist brought in on the case was a pleasant but severe person. She was impatient with the problem son, who laughed at the idea that he would be arrested again. He said, "Never again." Papo said, "You said that before, but its good to hear that since you're risking a long jail sentence." The therapist said, "Have you said before that you would never do this again?" Edwin replied,

"Yes, I have said this before but it's different this time. It's more serious." Papo said, "I think he does take it more seriously this time." The therapist said, "What would the family do to Edwin if he was arrested again? Everyone thinks he is going to slip and do it again." Papo asked Grandmother in Spanish what she would do to punish him if he smoked again. Grandmother replied (translated from Spanish), "I would be very disappointed." Papo said, "But what would you do, what would you do?" She replied, "I would be upset." Edwin interrupted and said as he had so many times in the past, "I'm not going to smoke again, so don't worry." Papo said, "I worry after this discussion." The therapist said, "I think everyone in the family needs to come in to see what can be done about this."

> **The family should take charge and impose a serious consequence rather than having law enforcement do so.**

The next week the whole family came in, feeling they had to do something. The therapist's goal was to persuade them that they had to do something. When the issue was raised, the younger brother said, "If you smoke again, I'll kill you." They all laughed about this, but it was a serious laugh. The sister, Pepita, said forcefully, "If you smoke again, I'll put your things out on the street. You won't stay in my house." In this way it was discovered that Edwin was living with his sister and her husband. The grandmother said in Spanish, "We need something serious to stop this." Papo said, "Let's agree on what we'll do as a consequence." Pepita said, "We can refuse to speak to him for six months if he smokes again." They were all quiet at this suggestion. For a close Latino family not to speak to a member for six months and to be put out of the house was a severe punishment.

In the follow-up, Edwin did not get arrested again. The family group became the disciplinarian. The family made the addiction a serious problem and agreed on a consequence for the addict if he relapsed. The consequence served to unite the family and keep the addict clean. The goal of the therapy, regardless of ethnic group, was for the family to take charge and impose a serious consequence rather than having law enforcement do so.

Families dealing with addicts are often in serious situations, such as dealing with physical abuse by the addict, and the police are not available in some circumstances. A solution is that the whole family must organize to deal with such situations.

An Addict Beats His Mother

Mrs. Magellan had five adult children. Four brothers and sisters were living with their own families, but she was being abused by a fifth child, Leslie, her thirty-year-old son who had trouble leaving home, and who insisted that she give him money for drugs. When she refused, he would hit her. He told her if she reported the theft to the police, he would really hit her. He not only robbed her but humiliated her by insisting that he was in charge of her. Her younger daughter discovered that the abuse was going on and confronted Leslie. He said he had to have the money because he was addicted. The sister was afraid of him. When she talked to her mother, the mother said she couldn't call the police because her son would beat her. The sister called a meeting with the three other children in the family. They agreed to go to the house and force the brother out. When the four of them went there, they not only threatened the addicted brother with the police but told him they would personally beat him up if he did not leave the house and agree never to come back. The procedure was successful. Once again the family took the power to stop the abuse.

Drug use is serious and involves jail, deception, and destruction of life. A family has the power to do something about this problem; they need only to exert that power in an organized way. First the family must unite and develop a consequence sufficiently strong to deter the addict from bad behavior. They must be firm and decisive when enforcing the consequence, whether it involves banishment from the family, jail, or other equally severe consequences.

In summary, some very difficult problems seem unsolvable until the family realizes it is within their power to change an out-of-control young person. In the previous cases, the following actions were taken:

1. The family defined the problem as a behavioral problem, not as a medical problem, so that they could deal with it.
2. The family planned an intervention using other family members.
3. Family members agreed on a plan.
4. Family members established consequences if the misbehavior continued. Possible consequences include:
   a. banishment from the family for a period of time
   b. staying at home together for twenty-four hours
   c. bringing in the law

Chapter 5

Leaving Home

There are young people who behave in unusual and bizarre ways. They talk to imaginary people, or behave in agitated or seemingly random ways that frighten people. Some wander the earth. These young people have two extremes. They make trouble or are they helpless or passive and do nothing. At either extreme they bring police and other agencies into their families. What is characteristic of such young people is that they are failures. They do not support themselves. They do not train successfully for a career. They do not form intimate relationships and therefore do not develop a normal social base outside the family. They are professional failures and their families must remain involved with them if only to reject them.

The term "mad" can be used for some young people although it has an unfortunate history of some bad connotations. Another term which might be used is "eccentric," which sounds too casual for dealing with young people who can be savage. The average young mad people who populate psychiatric wards, juvenile halls, drug rehab centers, and jails cause trouble in the community because of their mad and eccentric ways. Young people cause family

---

The introductory section of this chapter has been reprinted with some modifications from Haley (1997), *Leaving Home: The therapy of disturbed young people* (2nd ed.), New York: Brunner/Mazel. Reprinted with permission of the Taylor and Francis Group, LLC.

Directive Family Therapy
Published by The Haworth Press, Inc., 2007. All rights reserved.
doi:10.1300/5883_06

instability. To avoid argument, it should be conceded at once that there are organic problems which require medication in some cases. This work is about the average young person who has experienced mistreatment and some of them have been abandoned by their families.

At one time it was theorized that a young person behaved bizarrely surprisingly often at the moment of success which ends in failure. This was thought to be because of his or her fragile nature and inability to tolerate responsibility. A cause of a difficulty was thought to reside inside of somebody, not in relationships with others. In the 1950s when families were brought together under observation and within a concept of systems, it was noticed that a young person who behaved in a bizarre way could be described as responding to peculiar communication within his family. As observation of families continued, it was noted that people communicate with deviant structural patterns. For the first time it was noted that problem behavior could have a positive social cause. . . .

When a young person succeeds outside the home, it is not necessarily a matter of individual success. He simultaneously disengages from a family or social situation. In some form he leaves home. . . .

A family can be in real trouble when a child leaves home. There is one way the family can stabilize. The child can stay at home. The young person may stay at home for months or even years but the expectation increases that the offspring will have a life outside the family and the family and other relatives will be left facing each other. Another way the young person can stabilize the family is for him to develop some problem so he must stay home. It is not that he is intrinsically sick but attempting to protect the family from worrying about their own difficulties. . . .

In essence the therapy approach is like an initiation ceremony. The procedure helps parents and offspring disengage from each other so that the family does not need the young person as a communication vehicle, and the young person establishes a life of his or her own. Two extremes have often failed. Blaming the parents as a noxious influence and sending the young person away from the family typically fails. The young person collapses and comes back home. The opposite extreme—keeping the young person at home and attempting to bring about harmony between child and parents—often fails. This is not a time to come together but a time of disengagement. The art of the therapy is to bring the young person back within the family as a way of disengaging him or her for a more independent life (Haley, 1997).

Some problems require an expert because of special needs in the case. The following cases will give families some ideas for dealing with their out-of-control teens' serious problems. The ideas stress viewing the problem teens as normal people capable of handling normal situations at school or work. They can act politely instead of rudely. Serious problems need to be dealt with and can often benefit from a simple approach.

Father Gets Firm

When George went off to college, he began to behave strangely. He said he had a mysterious pain, and he was hearing voices and taking drugs, was not getting along with his friends, and was very withdrawn. He was hospitalized three times and medicated with a diagnosis of schizophrenia each time. The psychiatrist discharged him home for his parents to deal with the problem. When he was home, he lost control and broke the door down in his parent's bedroom. They called the police and the policeman and father persuaded George to go back to the hospital. They told him if went in voluntarily he could leave when he wished. When he wished to leave the next day, the psychiatrist said he was schizophrenic and needed to be locked up. He told the psychiatrist that he was told he could leave if he went in voluntarily. He then ran for the elevator. Several aides tied him to the bed and medicated him. The father brought another psychiatrist over to get his son released. When the two psychiatrists spoke together, the one said, "You are very courageous, because this boy has tardive dyskinesia, which is an irreversible side effect of antipsychotic medication." George was released home.

Therapy was started to get him to go back to college. The therapist* did not emphasize his crazy behavior but rather persuaded his parents to put pressure on him to return to college, which was appropriate for him at his age. The young man was alternately passive and active and aggressive. As he waited to go back to school, he dated a girl, which was unusual for him but appropriate for his age. His father was a scholarly man who tried to understand his son even if that antagonized the boy. He was quiet and withdrawn and fond of George. As the return to school approached, the family began to be agitated and differed on how to treat George. Mother and Father began to have conflicts with each other. The boy in turn became more agitated. This behavior coincided with him reserving a place in the dormitory at college. George said he would not go and insulted his father and mother. The father stopped being passive and insulted the young man. The therapist encouraged this behavior, indicating that the father could take charge if need be. When George got insulting, he pushed his father too far. The father began to threaten to expel George from home and cut off his money for college. George then began to placate the father and contacted the school to arrange a place for him. Father insisted that the boy behave himself and be polite.

George had difficulty adjusting to this stage of the life cycle of leaving home and it took several people to help him to normality. One would expect children to help their parents and support them; it is difficult to think that negative behavior might be something positive. However, it can be in the way it draws attention to the child's problem, which can help parents with their marriage diffi-

---

*Neil Schiff, PhD

culties by making them once again focus on the child, and not their own situation. Parents might not like this view because they may feel that it implies the problem is their fault, but it isn't. Fathers should be firm so that their kids can leave home successfully.

In the follow-up, George did well and six months later the parents separated despite the therapist's attempts to hold them together. George graduated from college and five years later he was still a successful teacher. Over the years, when George returned from his job, he would have lunch with the therapist. He has had a successful follow-up for more than twenty years (Haley, 1997).

Focus on one issue of normal behavior and insist that the client do the prescribed task.

The important step for parents in this situation is to agree on a goal for the young person and the steps to get there. The parents in this case focused on one issue of normal behavior and insisted that the young man do what needed to be done. This puts someone in charge and keeps the teen from being irresponsible. Most important, they stood firm in not accepting any insulting behavior and established consequences to back this up. What worked was the father taking a firm position that he and his wife would not be insulted or they would stop support. Rather than thinking of his son as ill, he thought of George as a misbehaving son. Father insisted that the young man behave himself and be polite.

Delusions

Marjorie, the oldest of eight children, began to run wild. She began to be irresponsible with her boyfriends. She slept with her boyfriend on the dining room floor. She was hospitalized at the university psychiatric ward because she was having delusions that two of her fetuses (she was not pregnant) were locked up some-

place and they would not let her have them. She smoked marijuana. She was also hearing voices. She was diagnosed as schizophrenic.

As was customary, when Marjorie was coming out of the hospital, the whole family was brought together. She said she didn't belong in the hospital and rudely said Father was wrong about her
misbehavior in high school. The family was persuaded she should
be back in school and not wasting her time in the mental hospital.
It was after this interview that the family realized that Mother was
withdrawing and as the oldest, Marjorie was being burdened with
all the children. The therapy focused on Mother, too, who also felt
burdened with eight children. When the parents threatened to split
up, Marjorie threatened suicide, fearing she would be in charge of
the eight children, whom she was fond of and worried about. The
therapy focused on getting Marjorie out of the marriage quarrels
and required her to go back to school and back to work at her part-
time job and not be a mother prematurely.

> **Reacting in a normal way can encourage normal
> behavior by showing that you think the person is
> capable of being normal.**

Marjorie graduated from high school. The parents separated finally and the children remained with Father. The therapy had focused on the girl not being mother to all those children. Mother returned in a few months and wanted to see the therapist and get his
opinion on the situation. The therapist told her that Marjorie was
doing well and the other children were being adequately taken
care of by Father.

Many families with a delusional teen who was hospitalized
would understand this problem as the offspring being sick. They
would not imagine that there was some dynamic in the family that

could cause such far-out behavior. The metaphor of the twin fetuses was never brought up in the therapy. If the therapist does not necessarily comment, the client will be more willing to express important ideas more freely. The focus of the therapy was getting the family to insist that the daughter get back to work or school to be productive if possible. Reacting in a normal way can encourage normal behavior by showing that you think the person is capable of being normal.

The Addict

Estelle was a heroine addict in her early twenties. She came into therapy with her mother and her father, who was reluctant to come because he was so angry at Estelle about breaking her promise not to use heroine again. At first, the father refused to speak to her in the session because he thought it would be forgiving her for her addiction. A goal was to get them to talk together. Estelle had been in a rehabilitation program and shot up there. They discharged her. The girl left home, simply walking out of the house and disappearing, which upset her parents. They hunted her down on the street and after two months found her and brought her home. Father and Mother were angry but hesitated to discipline her because she would disappear. This sequence of relapsing after attempts at rehabilitation occurred again and again.

Bringing Everyone Together

This session was a new attempt to have a family orientation to the treatment. They felt they couldn't do anything about Estelle's drug habit but came in when asked by the therapist. Her two brothers also came in. They had not been speaking to her but for this session, they did. The younger brother not only spoke with her but took her to the movies. The older brother, who lived out of town, said he was willing to take her into his own house. The therapist discouraged this because she felt Estelle should resolve her problem at home in the family. Living with Brother would not deal with the problems of Father and Mother, which were assumed to be related to the addiction. The therapist convinced the parents that they had to keep Estelle off drugs one way or another. The daughter was worried about her father's health; he was overweight. They made an agreement if he lost weight she would not take drugs. Estelle began to take care of her appearance. She joined a gym to lose weight. She went back to school and she bought herself some new clothes. Every summer the family usually went to the beach. This year Estelle did not want to go, saying she had a lot of schoolwork to do. Father said he would not go to the beach without her. Mother said, "Why not? We can go together." Father said, "I won't go without her because she needs supervision." Mother said, "Why not?" Father said, "She needs guidance with her addiction." This aroused Mother's jealousy who felt Father was too close to the daughter. Estelle ended up staying home alone while the parents went to the beach. She didn't shoot up.

> **In life-threatening situations, family members can make pacts with each other to change symptomatic behaviors.**

The therapist was moving to another state. She held a session with Estelle to tell her she was leaving and was worried about Estelle relapsing because she was so fond of the therapist. The supervisor said that if the case is successful she will survive the therapist leaving.

The outcome appeared to be good with this family. In a one-year follow-up, Estelle was married and apparently off drugs. She was going to school. As Estelle improved, Father and Mother became more amiable toward each other and looked forward to becoming grandparents.

Parents have power even if they think they don't. It is often possible in the case of addiction to involve the entire family, restructuring them to allow new ways of communication. They will often come up with answers to help the addicted person.

It is often possible in the case of addiction to involve the entire family, restructuring them to allow new ways of communication.

Panic Attacks

Saul was a young man who was hospitalized in the Veterans Administration Hospital for a nervous condition. His parents would visit him in the hospital. He had an unusual behavior when his parents came: He would faint. When this happened, his father would telephone an aide, who would come down and tell him to get up, and he would get up and go back to the ward. Saul said he was too anxious to stay with his parents for any length of time. The therapist took him on as a patient because of this peculiar behavior: He was interested in his fainting as a form of communication in the family. The therapist was trying to get him to venture outside the hospital without being too nervous. One day the mother and father came in to visit Saul and he talked without fainting. The mother said, "I have something I would like your opinion on. Saul sent me a Mother's Day card." "How nice," said the therapist. The mother said, "There's something wrong with this card." Father said, "It was just a mistake," placating Mother, who was clearly getting angry. "Show me this card?" the therapist asked. Mother took it out of her purse and showed it to him. The card said, "You've always been like a mother to me." Mother said, "There's something wrong with this card." Father said, "It's just a card," obviously attempting to placate Mother. Mother said to Saul, "Isn't there something wrong with this card?" Saul began to minimize the card by saying "It's just a card. They only had a few cards to choose from." Father said it's just a card. The mother said, "There's something wrong with it. I'm your mother." Saul began to apologize for the card without knowing what was wrong with it. Saul didn't faint. Mother had a powerful influence on Saul. As a trial to get out of the hospital, Saul was put in a foster home even though he was twenty-five years old. Mother came to visit the foster home and he was pleasant. She said to him, "How come you get along with that woman and you don't get along with me?" Saul fainted. That night Saul frightened his foster parents by getting upset and they sent him back to the hospital. Saul had trouble with his parents. He ultimately got out of the hospital and went back to his parents. When he was being discharged to the parents, Mother said, "I have allergies and you can't smoke in the house." Father said, "You can't make the house dirty." When they arrived home, Saul lit a cigarette and lay down on the couch, which Mother didn't like.

They slowly worked out their difficulties in family therapy. He didn't leave home and he made enough trouble so the parents had to take care of him. He stopped fainting and lived at home. Family therapy kept him from being a ward of the state.

Strange Delusions

This case is an exception; the idea of using the family will not work in all cases. Gretchen was a schoolteacher who complained of seeing dancing nudes over her head. She also said she saw a bear on the floor. Dr. Milton Erickson handled this case. He was careful to walk around the bear on the floor. The dancing nudes were so disturbing that she was going to quit teaching and become a ward of the state. She was transferred to another city and was without Dr. Erickson to deal with her strange ideas; when she left she would lose Dr. Erickson. He decided to solve this problem by telling her that she could put her delusions in a manila envelope and mail them to him. He would keep them in his office for her to visit them any time she needed to. She did this, and continued teaching and saw him occasionally. Dr. Erickson channeled bizarre behavior into socially acceptable areas—into a reality instead of a metaphor—to permit functioning.

> **Channel bizarre behavior into socially acceptable areas—into a reality instead of a metaphor—to permit functioning.**

Good and Evil Leads to Compulsive Behavior

Paul was a young Puerto Rican man who could not go to school nor hold a job because he believed that the good and evil forces within him were constantly fighting for control, and he could not stop walking. He would not sit down long enough to hold a job. In addition to psychiatry, and because his hallucinations were spiritual in nature, he tried every religious sect he could find to get help. In many countries, therapists who understand their own culture use informal healers as resources (Richeport-Haley, 1998a, 1998b). Paul was diagnosed chronic schizophrenic—undifferentiated type. His psychosis manifested in the belief that he was possessed by a demon that he first saw when he was six years old. His mother took him to a spirit medium, who advised her to take him to a doctor. She, however, relied on spirit mediums until he was twenty-three years old, when she finally took him to a psychiatrist. Paul used the spiritist explanation for his feelings of detachment, hand-washing compulsion, and refusal to touch people. He dichotomized the forces within himself into good and bad, with himself in the middle trying to keep the bad from predominating. To prevent the bad from taking over, he walked compulsively for hours and therefore could not hold down a job.

After two years in psychotherapy, the psychiatrist felt he could produce no change and referred Paul to another psychiatrist* for hypnotherapy. Paul continued to see spiritists at the same time. He returned to work and college. This therapist felt that "despite his progress, and since Paul was seeing mediums anyway, he would use a medium, Carmen, as a consultant to help banish Paul's demon." The therapist directed the interaction and then transferred the direction to Lao-tzu, Carmen's spirit guide. Lao-tzu located the "evil" in Paul's left hand and the "good" in Paul's right hand. Paul appeared very expectant as Carmen clasped his hands together and then pulled them apart sharply. Paul began to tremble in a contest between Paul's possessing entity resisting departure and Carmen's "vital fluid" working to push out the entity. Lao-tzu told Paul that he was "good, intelligent, and a normal man."

Concrete actions in a ritual context can banish symptoms.

The therapist resumed the direction of the interaction. As he thanked Lao-tzu for coming, Carmen, slowly recovering from the trance, asked what happened. The therapist used the remainder of the time to reinforce the idea of the expulsion of the demon. Since then, Paul has been working full-time for many years and has girlfriends.

Depending on beliefs, concrete actions in a ritual context can banish symptoms. Some faith healers use similar techniques to these that can be successful.

---

*Hilton López, MD

Old MacDonald Absurd Therapy

Susan, a twenty-three-year-old daughter of a professional family, beat her mother up at regular intervals, usually when the father went off to work in the morning. The father, an engineer who worked most of the time, did not know how to prevent the daughter from abusing Mother. The mother would not call the police because she felt she was to blame and she did not want the public to know. When seen alone, Mother would say she would not take any action to stop it because they had a proper family. When Father was seen alone, he said he couldn't help what was happening. "It just shouldn't happen," he said. When Susan was seen alone, she smirked and treated the situation like it was unimportant. The therapist gave Father a serious talk on how being hit can really hurt the wife. The mother was not able to defend herself because the daughter was so strong. They had a son, but he was away at college getting his PhD and was not available to help. The problem daughter was not having success leaving home. She went away to college and came back. She went away to get a job and quit and came back. She was doing nothing while looking for a job.

The therapist in this case* saw the parents together and advised them not to allow this to go on because the mother could get seriously hurt. He persuaded the father not to let his daughter hit his wife. Could they have someone else stay in the house so they would not be alone? Typically people are not abused when they have guests in the house. The father didn't know anyone he could ask. The mother said that she could find someone since she knew more people. They came back to therapy the next week and the daughter had hit the mother.

The therapist made a plan to intervene in this situation. He had Mother come in alone. He had Father come in alone. He told Fa-

*Neil Schiff, PhD

ther, "I have a cure for this problem, an infallible cure." He was carrying a box. "I guarantee that this cure is wonderful." Father was puzzled about what was in the box. The therapist opened up the box and revealed a child's phonograph. "This is a miracle cure," he said, much to Father's astonishment. He smiled at Father and turned on the phonograph, which played, "Old McDonald Had a Farm." He stopped the music. "Will your wife enjoy this?" he asked. Father said, "Yes, she had been a teacher." He brought the wife in and played the song for her. They laughed together. Surprisingly, they stood up and danced together as the daughter walked in during this interview with a look of dismay on her face. The therapist directed Father to say to his daughter, "You shouldn't hit your mother." He gave the family these instructions: "You should put this recording on every morning at 7:00 a.m. before Father goes off to work." The next morning, the therapist called the house and could hear "Old MacDonald" on the phone at 7:00 a.m.

> ## Absurd interventions in difficult cases
> ## may create startling results.

In a follow-up, it was learned that the daughter had not hit the mother again. The son returned from college, and with his wife moved the daughter out of the home by finding an apartment for her. In one weekend, Susan was moved. She liked this and began to look more seriously for a job, which she found. Mother and Father continued more amiably with each other. This intervention involved gathering the family to support the daughter. The therapist was surprised at a shopping mall five years later when a young lady approached and said hello to him. It was Susan, who was working successfully and showed no interest in violence. Therapists should allow absurd interventions in difficult cases. Absurd interventions may create startling results. The therapist set up a guaranteed cure. The puzzling, light-hearted directive expelled the daughter from the parents' relationship in a kind way.

Family Therapy at a Distance

Sometimes a youth can be physically out of the home—even living in another country—but is so emotionally tied to the parents that he really has not left home successfully. This was true in the case of a young depressed man from the Middle East, Abdul, who was brought in for a consultation in a therapy training program. He had spent years analyzing his sadness. The therapist had tried many things to get Abdul outside with little change. He had been enrolled in medical school but now spent all his time playing computer games and having sexual fantasies. His father was a physician in the Middle East. The supervisor, Haley, assumed that the client was failing in relation to his family and suggested a goal of having Abdul communicate with his family by mail or telephone as a way of making a change.

> HALEY: Challenge him in such a way that he does something helpful for himself to prove you wrong rather than because you ask him to. If you said, I think you should write your father and say that you are getting quite interested in women here, you are going to be very surprised at his response. So why don't you write him a letter and I will help you write the letter. (Haley & Richeport-Haley, 2003, p. 54)

This trainee was in conflict between two supervisors and had a great deal of difficulty carrying out the plan to write a letter to the father. There were parallels between the client not doing any task and the therapist not being able to carry out a directive. The sessions focused on carrying out the directive to write a letter to the father, discussing the possible reaction of his parents, when he would mail the letter, the mail delivery to the Middle East, and Abdul's rebellion against his parents. He said that he did not believe in God, that his girlfriends were not from the Middle East, and that he came to the United States against his parents' wishes. After he mailed the letter, Abdul revealed his risky sexual behavior on the Internet and previous childhood abuse.

> **An innovative therapist will think of ways to incorporate the family even when they are not present.**

In the follow-up, we learned that the father was casual about the letter and did not even acknowledge it until his son asked if he received it. He attended therapy sessions for four months. In six months, he had returned to college. The directive approach forced Abdul to take action after so many years of analyzing and talking about his sadness. The directive to write his father a letter saying he was doing well was a paradox leading to change because he was challenging his father but doing so more positively. In many cases, a family is not available. An innovative therapist will think of ways to incorporate the family even when they are not present.

A Runaway Teen

Sarah was a fifteen-year-old girl brought in after some violence between her and her mother. She left high school and was running away with an African-American boy. She already had moved in with his family. The mother did not like this happening and Sarah thought that her mother was a racist. In response to the violence that had occurred, Mother said that she didn't like being in a fight on the street regardless of the racial situation. This was a family in which the mother had divorced and remarried. The handsome stepfather was uncertain how to behave with this daughter, who was a pretty blonde. The daughter was brought home after Mother fought with her in the street.

Stepfathers Need Authority

The therapist,* conducted a family interview to bring out the issues in the family. The stepfather was present in the interview and it was unclear how much authority he had in the home. The therapist made the stepfather's authority clearer, since the stepfather was very fond of the kids and wanted to adopt them legally. The therapist encouraged him to intervene between Mother and Daughter, which empowered the stepfather as he began to take charge. Mother also became more accepting of the African-American boyfriend and met him along with his mother. Soon the daughter began to date other boys.

This is an example of a stepfather intervention. The stepfather asserted more authority in the home, particularly when he didn't agree with his wife's actions. When Sarah began to date other boys, Mother was placated, and normal family living could occur. Stepfather and Mother decided that she was having too much difficulty with the daughter, so Stepfather was to have the authority in that area, thus alleviating the family struggle.

Sleeping All Day

Zach was nearly eighteen. He was on probation for stealing money from his parents. The judge told him that if he did not attend school and continued stealing, he would be tried as an adult at eighteen. Another major complaint was that he slept all day, stayed out all night, and at times took drugs. He was not going to school and he said he would run away and live on the street, which he never did. The parents were threatened by that possibility and

---

*David Eddy, PhD

did not feel he was capable of living alone on the streets. He also insulted his father. The father insisted that the mother get the boy up and out of the house to look for a job every day at 7:00 a.m. If he refused to get up, the mother was to spray him with a hose. She did this once and the son hit her, which brought the probation department back into the home.

When the parents in conflict pull together, kids who have been making trouble begin to behave.

The therapist dealt with the issue of the boy leaving home and persuaded the parents that their son was capable of leaving because he would turn eighteen in two months. Rather than being hard on the boy, the therapist told them all to have a good time together and even have Father serve the boy breakfast in bed. The parents were shocked with this suggestion, which was just the opposite of what they had been doing. The father thought it was hilarious and laughed about it in the session. They were reminded that they would lose this boy as he grew up. The parents decided to focus on their own pleasures without focusing on Zach. They took a cruise to the Caribbean for two weeks and when they returned, the boy became more responsible and started school again. He even got out of bed. He had received the parent's going away as abandoning him and faced the issue of losing his home. The expectation was that the youth would continue to improve now that he felt more confident about leaving home, which would be done with the support of his parents. This is another example of a family with parents in conflict and a young person making trouble as a way of bringing the family together. When the parents pull together, the kids begin to behave.

The therapist saw Zach two more times. He moved away from home to live with some friends. He finished his GED and went to work. He said he was happy. He left home successfully. The parents had been persuaded that the son was capable of leaving home. They were also persuaded to focus on improving their relationship. When they did this, the boy was free. Surprise was introduced by having the father serve the boy breakfast in bed, the last thing the family would have expected.

A Penance for a Suicidal Boy

Ted was threatening suicide. His family took him seriously because his older brother had committed suicide. Ted was hospitalized and on suicide watch, and therefore under constant observation. His parents were very upset. The therapist* dealt with this case by long-distance telephone.

The therapist asked the family what the older brother would have done if he were alive. Ted said his brother would have done wonderful things for people because he was such a kindly person. The therapist persuaded Ted and the parents to do the things in the community that the deceased brother would have done had he lived. Ted and his parents thought this was a great idea. It helped Ted with the guilt over his brother's death and it benefited the family and the community. The young man wanted to be discharged from the hospital so that he could fulfill a contribution of his deceased brother. He was released, and gave up his thoughts of killing himself. He made lists of what his brother would have done if he lived and carried them out.

*David Eddy, PhD

Chapter 6

Couples

To use a directive approach, it is best to hypothesize that marital relationships are based upon sequences of behavior that follow rules. For example, a husband will routinely behave irresponsibly. The wife will behave responsibly and she will complain about the husband being irresponsible. They will follow this rule whenever they communicate. Symptoms are the expression of a conflict of rules. A couple can follow rules that lead to pleasant experiences or they can repeat rules that create distress.

Marital relationships are based upon sequences of behavior that follow rules. Symptoms are the expression of a conflict of rules.

A popular theory in family therapy is that behavior causes feelings. For example, a therapist might say to a wife, "Have you noticed that you followed the rule that you complain and your husband will defend himself against almost everything you say?" The wife says, "That's true. He never pays any attention to me." The husband responds, "She complains and is dissatisfied no matter what I do." She complains, he defends himself, and then he withdraws. A goal is to change these rules and thus the distress. The goal is not to stop following rules, which is impossible, but to stop

Directive Family Therapy
Published by The Haworth Press, Inc., 2007. All rights reserved.
doi:10.1300/5883_07

following those that repeatedly cause misery, as is illustrated in the next case.

Fighting

Rose and José, a working-class couple in their thirties, fought all the time. They were not married but living together with plans to marry someday. They both had a history of alcohol and drug addiction. They had completed the twelve-step program and were clean, but still thought of themselves as addicts. In therapy, Rose complained that José did not communicate, did not want sex, did not show her affection, and made her very jealous. He said she was always complaining and did not recognize that he was busy. They were not having sex anymore.

Paradox can be effective in changing distressing rules. The challenge is to change the rules so that the clients' emotions will change. To do something about Rose's complaining, the therapist in training was first advised to give the couple the paradoxical directive of asking them to do what they were already doing. It was evident that the rule they followed was that she complained and he defended himself, so they were asked to do that on command. Next the therapist attempted to change the rule by giving them an opposite directive of what they were doing. The therapist was told to ask José to criticize Rose, and ask her not to respond. Since they were avoiding sex, another paradox was proposed. The therapist said, "To get a better understanding of your attitudes about sex, it's forbidden to have sex this week." When Rose and José came in the next week, the therapist was instructed to say, "One thing I would rather not talk about this week is sex, because that is a person's private life." The result was that they resisted by talking about the sex they had during the week. Paradoxical directives to reverse their rules of Rose complaining and José objecting and then withdrawing were continued. The therapist was instructed to "Ask him to complain and her to defend herself."

> **Give the couple the paradoxical directive of asking them to do what they were already doing, and then direct them to reverse the rules.**

The couple was treated as normal, not as defective addicts. In the follow-up session, they reported they were having sex again, she was happy and not crying, and they were talking positively and joking with each other. The trainee therapist was surprised at how well the paradoxes worked. She told the group, "I'm amazed they were so happy. How did this happen? It was so different. I mean you should have seen them before. He was mad and she was crying. I'm trippin'. . . ." (Haley & Richeport-Haley, 2003, p. 247)

Unbalancing a Couple

A professional couple in their thirties had been married for seven years. As with many couples, the rule followed by this one was that the wife initiated contact and the husband responded. At a certain point in the marriage the wife stopped initiating and began to wait for the husband to do so. They talked in abstract terms and had been in long-term therapy. They were locked in a struggle and needed some action to destabilize them. The therapist needed to stop being neutral and elicit some action by bringing about a coalition. The couple was trying to decide whether to stay together or separate. Marriage therapy involves a triangle, and a couple changes when the therapist changes in relation to them. The supervisor suggested a plan that required the therapist to be unfair and not impartial. It was decided that the therapist would side with the wife, because the husband was not initiating and if he did so, it would please the wife. The therapist asked the couple to give therapy a chance for three months without separating. The therapist told the husband that he was all wrong—that he needed to court his wife and win her back. The therapist said to the husband,

"From what I heard tonight, you are really in danger of losing your wife. I think what you are doing is absolutely wrong. I think you are making a mess of things. You are doing things to turn her off— by not talking to her, by not being aggressive, by not seeking her out, by not courting her. I'd say you are absolutely wrong. It's your fault." Looking at the wife, he added, "And it's no fault of yours." The husband sat forward and protested, "I'm telling you, I think you're all b***s***." The therapist remained firm and convincing, answering each protest of the husband. "No," insisted the therapist, "You really have to go after her and court her." When the therapist unbalances this way, it is necessary to go to extremes.

> **Stop being neutral and elicit some action
> by bringing about a coalition.**

After this session they met again in two weeks. The therapist called the husband before the session and found out he was taking steps to please his wife. The husband began to buy presents for his wife, take her out to lunch, and call her. The husband's willingness to make the first move led to their decision to stay together and take steps to change their marriage. This technique forces the issue in couples contemplating whether or not to save their marriage (Haley, 1996; Haley & Richeport-Haley, 1998a).

The Secret Drinker

After three months of therapy focused on their son, the son improved but Sally and Sam began to have difficulty with each other. Sally's alcoholism was kept a secret within the family. Although everyone in the family knew she was drinking secretly, it became even more apparent when the son was no longer the focus of their attention. They decided to focus on the drinking issue. She had a special way to drink. She would wait until everyone was in bed except her and then she would drink bourbon until she fell asleep. She did this every night to the point of developing physical problems. The therapist* brought in Sally and Sam and had them acknowledge that Sally was an alcoholic. They were very proud and proper people who did not like to admit that Sally had a drinking problem.

The therapist persuaded them to agree that in order to help them with this problem he would have to use whatever means necessary. Sam said he would do anything to help his wife. The therapist told them to empty the house of all liquor. Sam did this. Sally said it would be hard for him to get rid of all the liquor in the house because he liked his wine, but he was willing to do it for her sake. Then the therapist proposed a more serious ordeal. If she took a drink, Sam would have to take off all of his clothes and be naked for twenty-four hours, whether or not anyone came to visit, including their son. Sam said that he could not do this; he couldn't be nude. Sally said, "That's true. He could never be nude." The therapist said, "Sam, you agreed to do anything and this will stop the drinking." Sam said, "There must be some other way to do this." The therapist said, "It is evident from Sam's reaction that this would be a powerful way to get Sally to stop drinking." Sam was caught between helping his wife and his shyness. The therapist stood firm and said, "We have an agreement, which starts now." The therapist wondered if they would have carried out this directive by the time he saw them the next week.

At the next interview, Sally had not had a drink. It was difficult, especially because they drank socially and liked to go bowling: "You can't bowl without beer." Sam didn't dare allow her to have a drink and she didn't dare have one. Both of them knew that they would carry out the task. They finally told their bowling partners that they were not drinking, and did the same with friends having wine at dinner. A few weeks later, still not drinking, Sally decided

*Neil Schiff, PhD

to take a week's vacation at a spa to lose weight and came back looking much better. She had never done that for herself before. Sally stopped drinking and lost weight. The couple threatened separation, which sometimes happens when a symptom improves. This family reaped a double benefit from therapy. Their problem son improved and Sally became—and stayed—sober.

If a person is in a life-threatening situation, absurd and embarrassing tasks often can be effectively employed.

After getting the couple to agree to do anything to get over the problem, an embarrassing task was arranged for the spouse if the drinker had one more drink. In this case, they kept to their bargain. One spouse can have a great deal of influence over the other's bad habits. If a person is in a life-threatening situation, absurd and embarrassing tasks often can be effectively employed. They should not be anything that causes harm. This ordeal for a shy and proper man was harder on them than the symptom.

The Anorectic Couple

Another example of spouses helping each other solve a serious problem is the case of a young wife, Matilda, a tall woman who showed up for therapy all bundled up in a big coat with her husband. She actually weighed 99 pounds and was painfully thin. She thought she was overweight and had tried to lose weight but was unsuccessful. She and her husband were in conflict over her weight, but neither of them knew how to help her gain weight and so they quarreled about it. The husband was unhappy with his wife's weight loss and was contemptuous of her eating difficulties when he had none, although he was gaining a little weight around the middle. He ridiculed her for not being able to put on some weight. They weighed each other and vowed they would get to their proper weight, which they specified.

The therapist,* put the focus on the husband's weight, instructing him to lose a pound for every pound his wife gained. This would show her that it could be done. They came in the next week and she had gained a pound, which she had planned to do, but he hadn't lost a pound as he had planned. He became exasperated with himself for not losing the weight, instead of with her for not gaining. In the following week, she followed the schedule of gaining weight and he didn't lose a pound.

> **Competition can motivate spouses to resolve problems.**

She continued gaining weight and stopped when she was a weight she had chosen as normal, which she had always feared she couldn't do. She had been angry with her husband for criticizing her and treating her like a child when she could not be the weight she wanted to be. When he stopped being interested in her weight, she stabilized at the weight she wanted. The husband was educated on the problems of gaining weight when she succeeded. He had to acknowledge that he had the same trouble she had in controlling his weight. Competition can motivate spouses to resolve problems. They can motivate each other to individually change by agreeing, "If you do one thing, I'll do another."

The husband and wife became more amiable with each other. She reached a desirable weight and he stopped nagging her about her weight. She realized she could be normal and demonstrated this to her husband. He was promoted to a very important job and lost interest in weight.

---

*Marcha Ortiz

The Guaranteed Cure: A Case of Bulimia/Anorexia

The problem had been going on for eleven years, since Kay was twelve years old. She would eat and throw up a maximum of twenty-five times a day with a minimum of four times a day. She found that she could eat whatever she wanted and just throw up. Kay was hospitalized when her weight dropped from 110 pounds to 70 pounds. She was dying. The therapist* saw Kay and her husband Don together. He had them first establish a critical weight and have a doctor available. She weighed 95 pounds at the interview and thought she was overweight. The husband thought a good weight for her would be 110 to 115 pounds. Then the therapist motivated them to commit to getting over this problem as a couple. He asked them, "From this day forward, do you want to get over the problem?"

Motivate clients by guaranteeing a cure if they agree to do the tasks you have assigned.

He obtained all the details surrounding mealtime: what Kay thought about beforehand, where she went when she ate, how she threw up, and how she knew when she was done. The fact that she described it so vividly showed she wanted to get over the problem. Kay described what she ate at yesterday's lunch after she bought her intended lunch of a little cup of cabbage. "I had a cheeseburger, french fries, onion rings, and a bowl of chili. When it was time to go, I ordered two cheeseburgers, one grilled cheese sandwich, two french fries to take them back to the office, and on the way I went to a liquor store, which is a little store on the street, and I bought four candy bars, a Twinkie, a bag of Fritos, and a Diet Pepsi." (Haley & Richeport-Haley, 1998b).

---

*Robert Kirkhorn

It took three interviews before a plan was made. Every aspect of the therapy involved the husband, who objected most to Kay's secrecy because they were very open with each other. The following directives were given:

Directive: I want you to keep a chart of how many times Kay vomits in a day.

Directive: Make a list of at least ten positive consequences if this problem were solved. In the next session they came in with two single-spaced, typewritten pages.

Directive involving lying and trust: Ask Kay not to weigh herself. Husband should weigh Wife and not tell her what she weighs for one week. Kay needs to be totally honest about how many times she throws up.

Directive: Did you ever tell her to cut it out if the plumbing backs up one more time? (They had a basement full of vomit.)

Therapist: I will give you two directives. One is minor and the other one will solve the problem.

Directive: Buy Kay lunch and you have two options. Either Kay eats everything or Kay can do whatever she wants with the food. The two of you can decide to throw away the food. This paradoxical directive is asking them to do what they were already doing. "Don, you be kind and gentle." Then the therapist said that he would guarantee them a solution if they did what he said, and told them to come back in two weeks. "If you are not ready to solve the problem, it's okay."

In the two weeks she vomited from four to seven times a day.

Directive: The therapist dragged out the discussion without telling them what to do to solve the problem. "Would you be committed to doing whatever it takes? You must agree not to tell anyone how the problem was solved." The couple expressed apprehension about what it could be and what they would have to do.

Directive: The next time you vomit, both of you give me a penny to do with as I see fit. The second time you vomit you give me two pennies. The third time, four pennies, the fourth time, eight pennies. The couple sees how it doubles. Eleven vomits could cost $1000 and if she continued, they could be bankrupt. They discussed the definition of vomit as either voluntary or involuntary. "Bring me the cash next week at 6:00 p.m."

The following week the couple gave the therapist $1.28. The husband said that Kay had a new outlook and had a new job. She got promoted and traveled on a business trip. The therapist saw the couple once a month for six months. Kay stopped vomiting and was more self-confident. The husband was more assured of himself. They enjoyed the humor in the shaggy dog story, which set up a consequence involving a geometric progression. The couple had the benefits of a good relationship with each other and solved the wife's eating problem together following the therapeutic directives. This case is a good example of motivating a client to follow directives.

Every Family Has an Uncle Charlie

Many families have an "Uncle Charlie" who can't stop drinking and his family tries and fails to control him. It became especially important in this family when his daughter was getting married. She sat down with her father and asked him not to drink on the day of her wedding and to be sober because she did not want her fiancé's family to know about this problem. He agreed. When the wedding day came he was absent and then showed up late. He walked in and fell on his face, drunk, in the living room. The family considered whether they should call off the wedding. His daughter and family finally forgave Charlie as they had done so many times before. They didn't seem to realize that forgiving him encouraged the behavior.

Family consequences can be vital to treatment.

Charlie always said that his relatives encouraged him to drink, while his wife said that she did not encourage him. As an example, they would drive home, and Charlie would say to his wife, "I could use a drink. Let's stop at a bar on the way home." His wife would say, "I won't have a drink. I'll wait while you have one." When Charlie was just finishing his drink, his wife would say, "I have the right to a drink, too. I'll order one." Charlie said that he just could not sit there while she had a drink and that was it; he got drunk. It takes two people to make a symptom and an addict can be determined by another person. The opposite is also true. An addict can be helped by another person. Family consequences can be vital to treatment. This case illustrates a family that did not impose any consequences.

Up the Nose (Cocaine)

Tomas fell in love at fifteen and wanted to marry Zelda as soon as possible. Her father, an upper-class landowner, did not agree that this young man, who was a lower-class Indian as far as the father was concerned, should court his daughter. Tomas spent his time pursuing Zelda anyway. Since her father forbade him to associate with his daughter, one evening Tomas even sat in the rain in front of her house anxious to see her. After a time, he left Central America for the United States and got a job working in a gas station, but sadly missed Zelda. He wanted her to be able to come to the United States and therefore worked hard. Not long afterwards, he was running the gas station and within a year was the owner. He managed to bring Zelda to the United States and marry her. The problem they brought to therapy was that, according to Zelda, he drank too much and was irresponsible. Then he began to take cocaine, and was soon addicted. Zelda threatened to leave him if he did not quit his addiction. She was worried about his influence on their two sons. In the interview, Zelda criticized Tomas and he defended himself, saying that he was keeping a business going. He said the cocaine did no harm. Zelda said it made him a poor businessman and that his company was losing money. Tomas's addiction cast him in a negative light in the eyes of his teenage sons. When he relapsed, they treated him with contempt, which was difficult for this proud Indian.

In the first interview, Tomas made it clear that he did not want to lose his family. He promised to give up cocaine and alcohol and Zelda insisted he do so. The therapist ended the interview by giving the couple tasks. As an example, they were each asked to write down all the good qualities of the other. They discovered good qualities in each other. In the second interview, Tomas came in high. Nevertheless, they had done their homework and smiled while reading the list of each other's good qualities. Tomas's brother, a recovering alcoholic, was also invited to the therapy session. Zelda was deciding whether to leave Tomas but she wanted to be fair and give him a chance. She also realized that she owned his company because he put everything in her name as a tax device. He was showing irritation that she didn't appreciate him. The younger son said Dad was "putting the business up his nose" because of the cocaine addiction. The manager was helpful to Zelda in keeping the business going. However, he was a little too helpful and was getting personally involved with Zelda. Tomas said this drove him to cocaine. The two sons responded that they wanted a successful company they could be involved in and they had trouble when their father was high.

In this case, a serious consequence was threatened by the family if the dangerous and unhealthy behavior of cocaine use was not discontinued. The therapist asked the family to come up with a serious consequence if Tomas took alcohol or cocaine again. The family never actually had to come up with a terrible consequence. Tomas and his brother attended AA meetings together. He stopped taking drugs and drinking. His wife and children treated him with respect. When this approach is used, often the threat of a serious consequence by the motivated family is enough to end addiction if it is not too severe. The mother was a powerful force to get her husband off drugs.

**Often the threat of a serious consequence
by the motivated family is enough to end addiction.**

Extreme Jealousy

Arnold and Jen, a tough-looking biker couple in their thirties, came to therapy with a serious problem. He had beaten her and it wasn't the first time. They both had sad and abusive histories and could talk about them very openly. The husband said, "My wife is having an affair, although she denies it, and I don't want to kill her." He was not joking.

"I want you two to talk reasonably. I want to hear from each of you what you think the situation is," the therapist said. This is a good example of how people talk when compelled to explain their difficulties.

Arnold's Side of the Story

ARNOLD: I can stop my drinking, which I've done, but my jealousy is another thing. . . . The way the situation is getting, it is probably time we get a divorce now. If she has to go to other men and sneak around behind my back for advice, there's just no way. Everything too entangled with my business with her "friend" with my business. She's very unhappy because she can't talk to her "friend" now, but she's really put in a bad position. She said if it was going to work out, we had to work it out between ourselves. I'm not going for a separation. That's what she wants. Once I start down that road and once I went through that much pain, I'm not gonna come back no matter how hard I try; I'm not gonna police her. She knows what it does to me. She knows all I ever cared about was her. After my parents got divorced, after that I never cared. It was like the end of ever having a family again. You don't want to get back in that position so you get hurt again. You put up that wall. You just want to believe in somebody really bad, but at the same time you are looking for flaws, and when you find something you kick yourself for believing they were perfect. You're just left alone and love them so much, that's why I'm so jealous. Honesty is so important to me. You just don't sneak around corners. There's this terrible attraction. She's blaming me and she hates me that her friend won't talk to her anymore. She did that to get back at me. Why not just f****** leave instead of getting back at me?

Jen's Side of the Story

JEN: I just don't know what to do. We've been together for fifteen years and been married for twelve. He can't stand being suspicious all the time. If this is the only way he shows his love, he can show it to somebody else. That's why I work with him, go home with him. I feel like I'm being suffocated. I hate it when he gets like my father. I'm an illegitimate child. My father sexually molested me when I was very young and beat the hell out of me. He reminds me of my father. This constant breathing over my shoulder. I can't have girlfriends. He says that's how I meet boys. He doesn't own me. I have feelings of my own. I don't want to give it up but I can't live like this. I don't feel that every motion of my body is to get a guy. That's what I get from him all the time. When he was 16 and I was 17 he kept after me. Some kids gave me a ride home.

ARNOLD: Finally she admitted, "I did ride home with those guys," and I smacked her and ever since then I've been this a****** sitting here.

Their attempts to solve the problem failed. He kept her at his side and was suspicious wherever she went. She made him suspicious and became angry at him.

THERAPIST: What is wrong is you have such an intense love. All you have is each other. The love you have is so intense it is like a cancer. You need to learn to love each other a little less.

The husband reacted, "Maybe I'm crazy but I don't think we love each other enough." The wife agreed.

Couples in intense situations need to change their distance from each other, gradually building trust.

You could interpret this case as the wife feeling neglected and hence making him jealous, and he would activate, thus risking her life. A logical solution in therapy was a series of steps leading them to love each other less. Step-by-step, she was allowed to go out to lunch alone. She could drive home from work alone and meet him at home. She could stay home from work at times since he owned the business. Couples in this intense situation need to change their distance from each other, gradually building trust. Since neither one wished to harm the other one or divorce, they started out by doing everything together and separated little-by-little until they were comfortable with each other. The therapeutic directives were designed to create distance between them in increasing increments.

The couple became more amiable with each other by adding some space step-by-step under the guidance of the therapist. Jealousy is a powerful force, as we will see in the next case.

A Penance for Jealousy

Faith healers provide an example of how a ritual can function as an ordeal or a penance to help people solve their problems. A man once brought his unfaithful wife to a Puerto Rican faith healer in New York and said he did not want to kill her. He asked the faith healer if anything could be done. The faith healer carefully examined the wife and concluded that she, herself, had not had the affair but that the spirit of a previous wife was responsible for it. He gave the couple a firm directive to travel a long way by bus, to a certain town in New England. They were to walk one mile outside that town to a certain tree, in front of which they were to perform a ceremony he had taught them. This ceremony was to exorcise the spirit of the previous wife. Then the couple had to make the long expedition back to the city. Performing the prescribed behavior was a penance therapy for both spouses, which rid the couple of their problem. Regardless of whether you believe in spirit possession, a ritual that is usually arduous enough, such as a pilgrimage, can be devised and carried out to overcome the problem.

A ritual can function as an ordeal or a penance to help people solve their problems.

The Wife Who Is Afraid to Leave the House Alone— Using a Symptom to Control the Spouse

Ginny had not left the house in years. She was afraid to go out alone without her husband or her mother. Her husband was becoming exasperated with her because he had to do all the household activities. He had to shop and take the kids to school and do the errands. The husband decided to take her to therapy to do something about it. His attempts to get his wife to go out alone failed because she would become too frightened.

They came into therapy together and were persuaded to follow a directive. The next day that the husband went to work, he was to tell his wife to stay home. The next morning when he went to work he told her to stay home. They thought it was funny and laughed. The second morning he told her to stay home. It wasn't quite so funny. On the third morning, she went to the grocery store alone for the first time in seven years. When the husband saw she had gone out, he was upset. "Where will she go if she starts going out alone?" he thought. She replied, "I've always said, if I could leave this house, I'd leave with my suitcase in my hand." From then on she went out alone. With adjustment they stayed together.

The paradox of telling someone to do what they are already doing seems very simple, but it can have a profound effect. Anyone can make this plan; whether it is carried out is another matter. In this case, the couple carried out the paradoxical directive. Doing so made them aware of the wife's reason for staying home.

> **The paradox of telling someone to do what they are already doing seems very simple, but it can have a profound effect.**

Affairs

Philip came in with his wife, Susan, because he believed she had had an affair. There are many kinds of affairs. They range from happening once at a party, to regular, covert affairs, to multiple affairs that do not disrupt the marriage. Susan complained that after a hard day's work she would come home and her husband would criticize her and offer no help around the house. He knew she was having an affair and expressed his resentment by not helping with the household duties. They quarreled a great deal and at first did not acknowledge that their arguing was because the wife was having an affair. Not only was she having an affair, but it had been going on for months and was one in a string of affairs. They did not want to separate, but neither one would admit it.

The therapist obtained an agreement from the couple that from this day forward, if either one of them was even suspected by the other of having an affair, they must separate immediately without comment. In other words, both suspicion and accusation are eliminated from their marriage. The couple accepted this plan, which was simplified to "Either behave or leave each other." This device often works because it gives couples an excuse to stay together. They can try it out as an experiment, with one of them pretending to have an affair, and then they would have to pretend to separate to see the consequences.

Shyness in Sexual Matters

Many young people have difficulty talking frankly about sex and sexual techniques. With couples who do not feel comfortable talking about sex, it is helpful to use metaphors so they don't have to speak directly about sex. For example, one way that Dr. Erickson dealt with this shyness was by using dinner as a metaphor for sex. He would say to a couple, it is important that you enjoy everything in life, including having dinner together. You should be concerned with each other's appetites and interests. Dinner should be pleasurable. You should not just have it anywhere in the house but in the appropriate place. You should have appetizers that you enjoy, and not dive right into the meat and potatoes. There should be a period after dinner where you relax with each other in the privacy of your own home. Without ever talking about sex explicitly, the couple can communicate politely and begin to speak more frankly, which later can turn into a discussion of sex.

Family Therapy with Multiple Personalities

This was a popular diagnosis not long ago but is less so today because of the false memory controversy, which questions whether therapists can implant false memories in clients to suit their expectations. There were two main approaches used with multiple personalities, which is called Dissociative Identity Disorder in the DSM-IV (American Psychiatric Association, 1994). One was to fuse or integrate the personalities and eliminate them. In the other approach, used by Milton Erickson, clients are encouraged to slowly and carefully confront the primary personality with the realization that there are other personalities in the same body. They are taught to communicate and collaborate to eliminate amnesia. One female client in her thirties had a serious problem with amnesia, waking up in places and not knowing how she got there. She had been severely abused as a child, had been hospitalized repeatedly, and was suicidal at times. Haley supervised an experienced therapist* in the use of hypnosis to bring out the different personalities in the session, and to have them identify themselves and become aware of one another, in order to control the amnesia. This was a complicated process because of the rapid switching from one personality to another. The therapists were bewildered by the changing personalities. Haley had the therapist develop a plan so that the internal personalities and the family members did tasks together. The husband attended the therapy sessions with his wife. He believed the "alters" were different moods of his wife and were not pathological. The therapy introduced the husband to his wife's alternate personalities and taught him how to struggle with them so that amnesia would not limit her functioning. In the sessions, she would receive different personalities while being held by her husband, who would talk to each personality and explain to it that we were not trying to get rid of it. Later the couple's foster chil-

---

*Randy Fiery

dren were brought into the sessions and learned what the situation was. Since the wife had been suicidal, the couple was threatened with losing the children, whom they loved dearly. This was an incentive for the wife to learn control over her loss of time. The outcome was that one of the foster children had a baby; the couple became foster grandparents and successfully helped rear the child. Haley, following Erickson (1939/1980, circa 1940s/1980; Erickson & Kubie, 1939/1967; Erickson & Rapaport, circa 1940s), took a very positive view of other selves, not necessarily considering them pathological but a curious fact of human existence. Doing directive family therapy with this problem is unusual and was successful in this case (Grove & Haley, 1993; Haley & Richeport-Haley, 1991b; Richeport-Haley, 1994).

Physical Abuse One More Time

The therapist expected a routine problem when he set up an appointment with this family. The mother had called and said that ten-year-old Ralph was having difficulties and she was worried about him. The whole family came in. The father was a nice-looking man, age thirty, in a business suit and glasses. The mother, son, and daughter accompanied him. The therapist said to the little girl, "Write your name on the blackboard so I'll never forget it." She happily did so and the brother did the same. As the family got comfortable, the mother appeared to be in distress, biting her lips and fingernails. "Are you upset?" Jerry asked. The mother replied, "Not much." The therapist turned to the husband and asked, "Is your wife upset?" "Yes, about this and other things." Talking to the husband, "Are there other things?" The husband replied, "We have family problems, financial problems, and I've been in three companies that have gone out of business the last year. When I want to relax I have to drink and that's terrible." While the wife sat with her head turned away, the husband continued, with his voice quivering, "You don't have a job, you don't have a family, you just don't have anything." The wife changed the subject and asked, "Can we openly talk about the children in front of them?" "Yes," said the therapist. "Ralph has problems relating to children his own age. He's afraid of them. He doesn't defend himself," said Mother. She asked if the children could wait outside. When the children were sent out, she said she wanted to leave her husband and had already filed for a divorce while she continued living at home. She was afraid because he talked about killing himself if she left. They had separated in the past, but this time she couldn't take it anymore. She remembered being terrified when he walked in the door drunk, took off his belt, and began hitting her with it, yelling, "One more time, one more time." The next day when I asked him why he did that, he said, "It was a way of expressing passion." She was terrified of him for thirteen years. The wife asked her husband, "Would you kill yourself if we divorce?" "Well, I did take those tranquilizers. I wouldn't care about any- thing. I would drink. I wouldn't work. There is no reason to live," he replied. The therapist told the husband, emphasizing the posi- tive, "Tell your wife you won't kill yourself." "Just deteriorate," said the husband. The therapist assured him, "We will slow it down." "I have feelings for him, the crying, and I feel sorry for him. But this it," said the wife.

For the safety of the wife and children, the supervisor decided to help the couple separate, because the wife had already filed for di- vorce. The therapist told the wife to pack her bags, leave the house with the children, and go to her parents' house so she would no longer be in danger. With the wife out of the room, he also told the husband this plan for separating. The husband became very agi- tated pacing up and down saying, "Oh God, if she left the house, Oh God." The therapist continued to encourage the husband to ac- cept the separation while reassuring him that he could handle this tough time. The therapist saw the couple together and they were both crying. The husband said to her, "I can do without sex, just continue to be there. I can change." The wife was firm, "I can't believe you could really change."

The therapist was left with the possibility that the husband would kill himself if the wife left. To lessen the pain on the first night, the therapist stayed with him for the evening, as a friend. The next day they all met in the office. The husband survived the first night. They negotiated the separation. The wife moved out. If the husband is suicidal, the therapist must think of hospitalizing him to protect him, but in this case, he opted to help him continue in his normal activities to earn a living and to accept the separation. The husband survived the divorce. One year later the husband had remarried. The wife had not.

It is important in cases of violence and where one spouse wants to separate to call the police if necessary, and for the couple to separate immediately to save a life. Often the husband has been hitting the wife over time and she has forgiven him. He minimizes the violence, but in this situation the helper has to maximize the threat of violence. Friends, family members, or neighbors can help them execute the separation successfully. They should not go back into the house together if violence is an issue. Friends, family members, or therapists need to be available for the suicidal spouse until he gets on his feet again.

Shoplifting

A woman was arrested for shoplifting when she took clothes out of a store. She couldn't stop shoplifting; it was just too appealing to her. But she did not want to go to jail; her family needed her. Afraid of being arrested, she struggled against her impulses and would walk through a store to the point of being frightened about it. She went to therapy when she realized she could be arrested at any time. She knew that the shoplifter had to carry the booty outside the store in order to be arrested. A therapist offered to help her solve this problem.

The therapist directed her to go to a department store and not steal, but go through all of the motions of stealing. She would pick up some clothes and put them down again. She would carry a box with something in it that turned out to be nothing important. She was amused when the security staff at the store followed her and suspected her of being there to steal. She discovered that the sensation she liked was the danger of being suspected of engaging in possible shoplifting behavior. No one could object, however, because she didn't actually take the goods outside the store, but ended up with the store detectives following her about, which pleased her. The compulsion to steal went away as she recognized what she was doing. This technique can also be used with other compulsions, such as addictions. The therapist should arrange for the client to perform the compulsive behavior up to the point of suffering consequences. As long as the client does not carry out the compulsion, he or she cannot be arrested. The mother's arrest would have devastating consequences for the family. In this case, carrying out a directive solved the problem.

Arrange for the client to perform the compulsive behavior up to the point of suffering consequences.

Summary

Except for the last case, the techniques in this chapter for marital distress involve a partner or family. First define the distressing rule in the relationship and try to make a change in the rule. For example, if one spouse complains and the partner defends himself or vice versa the couple may be persuaded to reverse this sequence, or to enact the sequence at a specific hour each day. This is creating a paradox, which works in mysterious ways. If one partner has an addiction that is destroying the person and the relationship, here are some techniques you can try: You can choose the action that would be most embarrassing for the partner without the problem, and if the addicted partner has one more drink, one more chocolate, one more smoke, the other person must do this embarrassing act. If one partner is having a serious problem with eating or drugs, they can make a contract that one will lose weight as the other one gains weight, or one will stop smoking if the other stops drinking. The family can arrange a serious consequence if the addicted person uses the substance or hurts himself once again. The family should mean it and be firm, because often the problem is a life-threatening one.

With issues of infidelity or even the suspicion of infidelity, one useful directive is to persuade the couple to make an agreement that if either one even suspects the other of having an affair, they will separate. Another technique is to direct the couple to stop loving each other too much. Have them free up each other's time so they are not together constantly. They can desensitize each other little-by-little and alleviate the feelings of extreme jealousy. A couple at their wits' end can perform a ritual, such as a pilgrimage to a site, or make an offering, or do a penance in church. In cases of physical abuse, the abusive person must be forced to leave the home; abuse should not be tolerated. The therapist must urge the family and the community to take immediate action to keep everyone safe.

Chapter 7

Retirement and Aging

Throughout the world many people do not have the financial means to retire and not everyone wants or needs to. Some people remain healthy and active well into their advanced years. This is true for many Okinawans (Weil, 2005), who are known for healthy longevity. Although we have not discovered the fountain of youth, many people do not want it. Aging brings with it many benefits. Women become respected in their families. Grandparents are taken care of by their children's families while sharing in all of the activities, and are asked for their wise advice. Artists continue to work. Musicians continue to play. Dancers continue to teach.

We returned to Bali in the 1990s to do fieldwork on cultural continuity in the village where Gregory Bateson and Margaret Mead lived for four years in the 1930s. We spoke to several elders who knew them. In Bali, the elders are protected in a compound where the rest of the family resides. The household is surrounded by a wall with the family shrines, a kitchen, and small apartments inside for different generations. You can see elders and younger family members preparing offerings and placing them on shrines to the gods, while young mothers bathe babies in the courtyard. Nobody is put away in a nursing home or assisted living. They remain at least spiritually active and productive. Elders continue to perform in trance dance ceremonies, as they have their entire lives, which gives them a sense of continuity, peace, and well-being.

Directive Family Therapy
Published by The Haworth Press, Inc., 2007. All rights reserved.
doi:10.1300/5883_08

Unlike other life stages that are marked by a specific event, in the United States and many other countries aging is not clearly defined; it is generally marked by the onset of social security benefits and other pensions. In the 2000 U.S. Census, 35 million people were older than 65 years of age and more than 4 million were older than 85 years. More often than not, nuclear families cannot care for aging relatives. Increasing life spans have resulted in many changes in the family. A 60-year-old woman can have a baby today with new technology. A 102-year-old can still boss around an 82-year-old offspring. People can be married for more than fifty years and still have marital problems. We know a woman in her nineties who works to support and take care of her elderly sick daughter. Retirement can free people to do what they want to do; however, if someone has lost a job and is alone, he or she may not know what to do.

The Wife Who Could Really See

Ethel and Charles were retired a short time. He had spent all his time helping his wife see doctors for vision problems. Charles brought his wife to psychotherapy because she could not see. The doctor who tested her sight concluded it was hysterical blindness. The couple became angry at the diagnosis.

People often develop symptoms to help one another.

People often develop symptoms to help one another. The intervention was to encourage the husband to work at his career. He had been a newspaper editor. When he retired he was at a loss and became depressed. When that happened, he began to take his wife's problems more seriously—it gave him a purpose. When he got another job in retirement, her eyes improved. "It was like a miracle," he said. When she could see, her husband became depressed and was at loose ends. The goal of therapy was to give him something to do. The problem was really the depressed husband and not the wife.

The Woman Who Claimed to Have the Worst Daughter-in-Law in the World

An elderly woman named Bernice went through all the worst aspects of growing old. Several misfortunes befell her and a therapist attempted to solve the problems. She complained that she had the worst daughter-in-law in the world who bad-mouthed her to her grandchildren, although in fact she had been discharged from her retirement community for aggressive behavior, something that was not easily arranged. She was very depressed and did not seem to have the desire to do anything. She tried going to a dance but fell down there and injured herself. As a result, she became more cautious in her movements. Her wallet and keys were stolen. This upset her greatly and made her unsure of herself. Living alone, she was lonely and would just look at the telephone. There was a man showing an interest in her, but she dismissed him. "Everything is a big deal for me." She lost her self-confidence after losing her wallet and keys and taking a fall. A crisis came when she sat down on the kitchen floor in her son's house and wouldn't get up. Her family finally got her up and out but they were reluctant to have her visit their house after this incident. Her son secured an apartment for her. She visited her other son who lived out of state to see if that family was a refuge. Instead, her two sons were pulling together to get her to behave.

Bernice had been referred to a psychiatrist, but ended up at a clinic instead because she couldn't afford the psychiatrist. She told the therapist* that this was the reason she was there. This statement could have prevented a positive view by the therapist but

---

*Richard Specter, PhD

he enjoyed doing therapy with older people and was very patient with her. He told her that everything is a step-by-step process. He concentrated on the smallest thing to make the change significant. Bernice recalled herself as an elegantly dressed woman who had held an important position in the labor union. She complained that she could not improve herself now. She had too many shabby clothes for many years and wanted to replace a few of them with new ones. The therapist encouraged her to go to Kmart and buy two new pieces of clothing and throw out two old pieces. The therapist shook hands on this commitment, which began a domino effect for Bernice. The next thing that occurred was that she was invited to her son's house on Sunday and "the worst daughter-in-law in the world" picked her up at her new apartment and drove her to their home. She made a nice fruit bowl to take for the meal and the family enjoyed the dinner together. Little by little she gained her self-confidence back and began to participate in more and more activities.

> **Ask the client for a commitment to do small, realizable tasks and compliment the person once each task is completed.**

The example of Bernice points to many of the problems of old age, including physical difficulties, loneliness, boredom with TV, and depression. The therapist dealt with each issue and insisted on a commitment from her that she would carry out the tasks they discussed. She bought some new clothes. She began to behave when talking to her son and his wife. She realized that if she did not cooperate with her son she would be forced to move to another state and live with her other son, whom she did not like.

To build an older client's self-confidence, a therapist can ask the client for a commitment to do small, realizable tasks and compliment the person once each task is completed. Little by little, the person will slowly make friends. It is important for the therapist to have the necessary skills to make small changes with older people who become habitual in their ways.

One should not assume that aging exhausts people entirely. There is the case of an active eighty-two-year-old grandmother who supported herself, her daughter, and two grandchildren. Her daughter resented her domination of the household, while accepting the money she provided. The objection was that Grandmother was working in a private practice as a successful prostitute. She insisted on being referred to as a "call girl." The granddaughter did not like to find the johns waiting in their living room. Many of them had been clients for years. Yet she and her children accepted being supported by Grandmother. Therapy was necessary to establish some house rules so that they could all get along more amicably, so that Grandmother behaved appropriately, and so that the family hierarchy was appropriate.

References

American Psychiatric Association. (1994). *Diagnostic and Statistical Manual of Mental Disorders DSM-IV* (4th Ed.). Arlington, VA: American Psychiatric Publishing, Inc.

Elkaïm, Mony. (1995). Entretien avec Jay Haley par Mony Elkaïm. *Resonances, 8,* Toulouse, France: Editions Systemes et Reseaux.

Erickson, M. H. (1939/1980). Experimental demonstration of the psychopathology of everyday life. In E. Rossi (Ed.), *The collected papers of Milton H. Erickson on hypnosis, Vol. III.* New York: Irvington Publishers.

Erickson, M. H. (circa 1940s/1980). The clinical discovery of a dual personality. In E. Rossi (Ed.), *The collected papers of Milton H. Erickson on hypnosis, Vol. III.* New York: Irvington Publishers.

Erickson, M. H., & Kubie, L. (1939/1967). Permanent relief of an obsessional phobia by means of communication with an unsuspected dual personality. In J. Haley (Ed.), *Advanced techniques of hypnosis and therapy: Selected papers of Milton H. Erickson, MD.* New York: Grune & Stratton.

Erickson, M. H., & Rapaport, D. (circa 1940s). Findings on the nature of the personality structures of two different dual personalities by means of projective and psychometric tests. In E. Rossi (Ed.), *The collected papers of Milton H. Erickson on hypnosis, Vol. III.* New York: Irvington Publishers.

Grove, D., & Haley, J. (1993). *Conversations on therapy.* New York: W. W. Norton.

Haley, J. (1955). Paradoxes in play, fantasy and psychotherapy. *Psychiatric Research Reports, 2,* 52-58.

Haley, J. (1962). Family experiments: A new type of experimentation. *Family Process, 1,* 265-293.

Haley, J. (1963). *Strategies of psychotherapy.* New York: Grune & Stratton.

Haley, J. (1964). Research on family patterns: An instrument measurement. *Family Process, 3,* 41-65.

Haley, J. (1967a). Speech sequences of normal and abnormal families with two children present. *Family Process, 1,* 81-97.

Haley, J. (1967b). Experiment with abnormal families. *Archives of General Psychiatry,* 53-63.

Haley, J. (1967c). *Advanced techniques of hypnosis and therapy.* New York: Allyn & Bacon.

Directive Family Therapy
Published by The Haworth Press, Inc., 2007. All rights reserved.
doi:10.1300/5883_09

Haley, J. (1968). Testing parental instructions of schizophrenic and normal children: A pilot study. *Journal of Abnormal Psychology, 73,* 559-565.

Haley, J. (1973). *Uncommon therapy: The psychiatric techniques of M. H. Erickson, MD.* New York: W. W. Norton.

Haley, J. (1981). *Reflections on therapy and other essays.* Chevy Chase, MD: Triangle Press.

Haley, J. (1984). *Ordeal therapy: Unusual ways to change behavior.* San Francisco: Jossey-Bass.

Haley, J. (1985a). *Conversations with Milton H. Erickson, MD, Vol. II, Changing couples.* New York: Triangle Press/W. W. Norton.

Haley, J. (1985b). *Conversations with Milton H. Erickson, MD, Vol. III, Changing children and families.* New York: Triangle Press/W. W. Norton.

Haley, J. (1987). *Problem-solving therapy.* San Francisco: Jossey-Bass.

Haley, J. (1989). The effects of long-term outcome studies on the therapy of schizophrenia. *Journal of Marital and Family Therapy, 15*(2), 127-132.

Haley, J. (1996). *Learning and teaching therapy.* New York: Guilford Press.

Haley, J. (1997). *Leaving home: The therapy of disturbed young people* (2nd ed.). New York: Brunner/Mazel.

Haley, J., & Hoffman, L. (1967). *Techniques of family therapy.* New York: Basic Books.

Haley, J., & Richeport-Haley, M. (Eds.). (1991a). *Milton H. Erickson, MD, In his own voice: Sexual behavior, the male* (50 min. audiotape). La Jolla: Triangle Press/ W. W. Norton.

Haley, J., & Richeport-Haley, M. (Eds.). (1991b). *Milton H. Erickson, MD, In his own voice: Erickson on multiple personality* (50 min. audiotape). La Jolla: Triangle Press/ W. W. Norton.

Haley, J., & Richeport-Haley, M. (1998a). *Unbalancing a couple* (35 min. video). La Jolla, CA: Triangle Press.

Haley, J., & Richeport-Haley, M. (1998b). *The Guaranteed Cure: A Case of Bulimia/Anorexia* (50 min. videotape). La Jolla, CA: Triangle Press.

Haley, J., & Richeport-Haley, M. (2003). *The art of strategic therapy.* New York: Brunner/Routledge.

Richeport, M. (1988). Transcultural issues in Ericksonian hypnotherapy. In S. Lankton & J. K. Zeig (Eds.), *Treatment of special populations with Erickson approaches (Ericksonian Monographs, no. 3)* (pp. 130-147). New York: Brunner/Mazel.

Richeport-Haley, M. (1992). The interface between multiple personality, spirit mediumship, and hypnosis. *American Journal of Clinical Hypnosis, 34*(3), 168-177.

Richeport-Haley, M. (1994). Erickson's approach to multiple personality: A cross-cultural perspective. In J. K. Zeig (Ed.), *Ericksonian methods: The essence of the story* (pp. 415-432). New York: Brunner/Mazel.

Richeport-Haley, M. (1998a). Ethnicity in family therapy: A comparison of brief strategic therapy and culture-focused therapy. *The American Journal of Family Therapy, 26,* 77-90.

Richeport-Haley, M. (1998b). Approaches to madness shared by cross-cultural healing systems and strategic family therapy. *Journal of Family Psychotherapy, 9*(4), 61-75.

Richeport-Haley, M. (2001). An anthropological view of Jay Haley's therapy. In J. K. Zeig (Ed.), *Changing directives: The strategic therapy of Jay Haley* (pp. 119-138). Phoenix: The Milton H. Erickson Foundation Press.

Richeport-Haley, M., and Haley, J. (1995). *Dance and trance of Balinese children* (50 min. video). New York: Filmakers Library.

Richeport-Haley, M., and Haley, J. (1997). *Whither family therapy? A Jay Haley version* (50 min. video documentary). La Jolla, CA: Triangle Press.

Scherl, C. R., & Haley, J. (2000). Computer monitor supervision: A clinical note. *American Journal of Family Therapy, 28,* 275-282.

Weil, A. (2005). *Healthy aging.* New York: Alfred A. Knopf.

Yapko. M. (1994). *Suggestions of abuse. True and false memories of childhood sexual trauma.* New York: Simon and Schuster.

Appendix A

Interviews with Jay Haley

AN INTERVIEW WITH JAY HALEY BY MONY ELKAÏM (THE EARLY YEARS)

ELKAÏM: My dear Jay, before you met Bateson and became part of the first Palo Alto group, what were you doing?

HALEY: I was a theater major at UCLA. I got a BA in theater and the last semester, someone posed the question, "Why do people go to the movies?" There were about 50 million people who saw a movie in those days. One big, popular movie would have that big a draw, so there must be something powerful to draw all those people. I got interested in that just as I left UCLA. Then I went to New York. I wrote for a year. I had sold a story to the *New Yorker* so I thought I was going to be a great success. I didn't sell another one for five years. But I went to New York for a year, and then I came back to California when my father died. I had the problem of what to do to make a living. I decided to go back to college as an English major, so I registered at the University of California. They told me that if I went to the library school for nine months, I could get a job. There were few librar-

---

Edited interview reprinted with permission from Elkaïm, Mony (1995), Entretien avec Jay Haley par Mony Elkaïm, *Resonances, 8,* Toulouse, France: Editions Systemes et Reseaux. Mony Elkaïm, MD, was Director of the European Family Therapy Association (1992–2001).

Directive Family Therapy
Published by The Haworth Press, Inc., 2007. All rights reserved.
doi:10.1300/5883_10

ians. So I got a degree in librarianship, and went down to Stanford; I studied mass communication to get my master's. While I was there, I discovered that Gregory Bateson was one of the few people who ever examined a film. He studied German propaganda films. So I went over to see him to talk to him about analyzing movies. He hired me on this project. We had an argument. He didn't appreciate the castration conflict in this German film where there was a very significant knife. I was pretty Freudian then, so I was correcting him. But apparently he liked it, because he hired me. He hired John Weakland at the same time, who was studying Chinese films. So all three of us were studying films. Bateson let me finish my master's degree while working with him, and that's how I got involved with him. We started just communication in general, paradox in communication, primarily animal behavior, and films at the beginning.

ELKAÏM: In what year was this happening?

HALEY: The beginning of 1953. Actually, he hired me as a secretary. I was a reference librarian at Stanford by then, and he paid me what they'd paid me at Stanford because he had this two-year grant. I had to decide whether to quit Stanford and go with him, with tenure of only two years, or stay where I was and become a librarian. I went with him, and was with him for ten years with no tenure. We got a grant from year to year, two years. It was precarious.

ELKAÏM: How old were you at the time?

HALEY: In 1953, I was 30 years old.

ELKAÏM: So you already had a family then.

HALEY: I had a pregnant wife and a child.

ELKAÏM: And, how was it? What was it like working with Gregory Bateson and John Weakland at that time? What sort of research were you doing?

HALEY: We were housed in the VA Hospital, but we weren't studying psychological material from the hospital; we were studying animals at the zoo, training guide dogs for the blind, and ventriloquism. Well, it was a mixed bag because Gregory was an extraordinary man. He was the major social thinker in that decade, and he was his own form of deviant. You know, he was never a professor. He was always a visiting professor. Nobody would hire him as a professor! The University of California made him a regent, which puts him in charge of the University on the board, but they wouldn't make him a professor. He had difficulties with anthropologists, because he thought differently than many of them did. As a research director, he was great. He posed us the problem of paradoxes in communication—that was his grant—and turned us loose really. So we could study anything that interested us.

ELKAÏM: And what interested you at that time?

HALEY: Well, I started on films and did a dissertation on a popular movie. Then I got interested in hypnosis. I met Erickson the same year; I took a seminar from him and began to study hypnosis as a form of communication. John Weakland joined me on that. Then in 1954 I was talking to a psychiatric resident who said, "If you're interested in communication, you should talk to this patient," so I started talking to the patient. Actually, the resident was trying to find somebody to take the patient over because he had to leave. So I started interviewing him and he was a word salad sort. He said he was from Mars, that his mother's name was Margaret Stalin. Nobody knew who he was. They picked him up walking down the street carrying a machete. They thought he was drunk, and when they dried him out, he didn't sober up. He wouldn't say where he was from. He said he was born on Mars and so they put him in the state hospital. He was there about ten years. He mentioned an Army serial number, so for the heck of it they looked it up and there was a guy named Earl Lane who had been in the Army for three months and who was kicked out on a psychotic discharge. I began to talk to Bateson about this man and we began to record him and listen to him. I was interested, and Bateson got interested in how he qualified things. He had trouble framing something as being real or not real, and we got interested in that problem. We started on a concern with perception, whether he could perceive correctly or not, which is the way people were thinking of schizophrenia then.

So they sent him over to the Veterans Hospital where I was. I began to talk to him. He had an interesting way of talking. He had an extraordinary skill with words for a guy who had a third-grade education. He was a migratory laborer, working out in the fields when he was arrested. For example, I asked him, "What's your mother like?" He said, "Skinny as a wolf, painted like a cat with a long tail like a scorpion which stings." That's with a third-grade education, so he was intriguing in many ways.

Then we shifted more to how this was a communication to somebody else; it wasn't just his perception. It was a metaphor which he was creating, and that got us interested in the metaphors of schizophrenia. The first grant ended in 1954 and we needed to raise some money, so we applied for a grant to study schizophrenia from the point of view of communication. We got the grant so we had two more years. What happened was that Bateson got a grant to study the paradoxes of communication. The way he got it was through a businessman who was head of the Rockefeller Foundation. Bateson went to talk to him about getting a grant and the man said "You have it." He immediately understood Bateson because he was in communication himself, and so he gave him the grant. Two years later, when the grant ended, we hadn't accomplished much in terms of any real production. We were exploring paradoxes, and Bateson went back to get this grant renewed when the man who gave it to him was no longer there at the Rockefeller Foundation. So Bateson was sure he was going to be turned down, and he went there and he was turned down. Norbert Weiner, the cybernetician, had been out to visit us and Bateson wrote him a letter saying that schizophrenia is caused by a person being punished for expecting punishment. He gave the example that parents will hit a kid, and then when the kid sees them again, he'll cringe. The parents will get angry at him because he's cringing as if he's going to be punished when he has been punished. And so he is expecting punishment. I think Bateson went back there expecting to be punished by being turned down on this grant, and he was turned down. So we then decided to write a grant on schizophrenia, and did. We were granted another two years with another foundation. I've forgotten which one. We were always with the smaller foundations; we weren't exactly accepted by the National Institutes of Mental Health and those places.

ELKAÏM: Jay, you wrote an article in 1958 in which you insisted on the fact that the double bind was something which was not happening between the mother and the child, but was like two people caught in a revolving door, a situation in which you don't know who is pushing who, in which you don't know what comes first, the chicken or the egg. For me, that article was very important because, until then, people had talked about double binds in terms of someone trapping, or binding, someone else. Did you have discussions with the whole group before you wrote that?

HALEY: We were together eight hours a day for ten years and had endless discussions, so you can't tell where an idea came from really.

We were into cybernetics and circular systems, and it was becoming obvious that the parents were bound by the kid as much as the kid by the parents. The first family I saw that was absolutely evident because the son, forty-three years old —the parents were in their seventies—sent his mother a Mother's Day card saying, "You've always been like a mother to me." The mother brought it into the session saying, "There's something wrong with this card." But obviously, she was in some strange bind that he would put her in by saying, "You've been like a mother to me." That takes some communication skill to do that.

ELKAÏM: That's very interesting. So that's one of the first families you saw yourself?

HALEY: It was the first. The whole project started then.

ELKAÏM: So were you the one who became interested in Erickson and asked Bateson to take a look at Erickson's work, or did he know him before?

HALEY: He knew him before.

ELKAÏM: He knew him before. Was he a friend of his?

HALEY: Bateson and Mead went to Bali on a field trip for about three years in a village there; they studied trance dances. They then consulted with Erickson about trance, and they showed him films of dancing and asked him to say when the person went into trance or not. Erickson hypnotized his wife and had her estimate it, too, on the theory that a person in a trance recognizes people in a trance more than one not in a trance. They got involved with each other at that time, and Mead became quite a friend of the Erickson family. When I asked Bateson if I could go take this seminar, I didn't know he knew Erickson. "What he said was, "I'll call him up and ask him."

ELKAÏM: I see. So Erickson hypnotized his own wife?

HALEY: Yes.

ELKAÏM: Tell me, you know that family therapy students learn about the discussion, or the disagreement, between you and Bateson on the subject of power. Could you please tell me, was this argument important when you were on that project?

HALEY: I had that interview with John Weakland, and neither one of us can remember the issue ever being discussed with Bateson in ten years! He never got unhappy about the way I was interested in power. I was writing papers which he was obviously approving because he was in the footnote on control in therapy and so on. I think what happened is that ten years later, after the project ended, he was being pushed to agree that therapy was a good idea and that power was important in it, and he didn't want that to be part of him. But the interesting thing to me is that there were two major therapists who were the most power-oriented people in the country. One was John Rosen, who forced psychotics down on their knees, and Bateson arranged that we study him and enjoyed him immensely. The other one was Erickson, who said, "It's best to take power when you're doing therapy" and Bateson was perfectly agreeable about that. So it never came up in the project.

ELKAÏM: So according to you, how did the discussion on power begin?

HALEY: Well, I think it came about after the project ended. Bateson really didn't like therapy, and he didn't like psychiatry, and he didn't like hypnosis. His project centered on those three areas, because he gave us the freedom to go into anything we wanted, and that's what we went into. He consulted on it, arranged it, and approved our going into it. When we started doing therapy, Bateson didn't like to do therapy himself. He was an anthropologist and so doesn't believe you should change your data. You should just examine the data. In therapy, you have to change the data, you're trying to change people and you're trying to do it deliberately. He didn't like that. He didn't mind if somebody else did it, but he didn't want to do it himself. So he would do a therapy where he hoped people would get better spontaneously, or he would lecture them, but he wouldn't do "A" to get them to do "B" or do any manipulation of any kind. I think he had been in Jungian therapy, and that had an influence on him.

ELKAÏM: So, he saw patients himself, individually and in families. How was he with patients?

HALEY: Well, he had a group of alcoholics which he studied and he did therapy with them. He was very dedicated to those guys.

He'd go and bring them back to the hospital when they were found drunk out in the street. He was a very concerned, and a humane man with them. But he didn't really do therapy with them in the sense of setting out to change them. He did not use an Erickson procedure where he might paradoxically do something with an alcoholic. Bateson would be as straightforward and as rational as he could. He had two kinds of patients: one set was these alcoholics; the other was when we all started seeing schizophrenics. We did a survey of all the schizophrenics we could find and did a whole series of interviews on their first break, on what flipped them out. One of the interesting things to me is that the whole field at that time said the past causes the present, and when he posed the double bind, it was a product of childhood experience. It was the past. Somehow we made the shift to arguing that schizophrenic behavior was adaptive and appropriate to the present, which is what family therapy argues: that a person's symptoms are appropriate in the present social situation, and that's why you have to change the social situation. Bateson had no problem with that. He made that shift from childhood to current life with no problem. I think it may be his anthropological background.

ELKAÏM: So Jay, you were also seeing families at that time. What interested you then in the families you were seeing?

HALEY: There were a lot of new things all at once. I saw my first family because my patient, a forty-three-year-old, who sent his mother a Mother's Day card, felt he couldn't leave the hospital unless he went home with his parents. He couldn't go somewhere else. Yet he couldn't stand being with his parents for more than about five minutes or he would fall down on the ground in the hospital, and they would call an aide who would come and take him back to the ward. I was seeing him individually, and it seemed to me that if he was going to go back home, he couldn't go back home if he was so scared he couldn't be with his parents for five minutes. So I brought his parents in to see why he was so scared of them. He stood up against the wall like Jesus, but he stayed in the room, and we talked for an hour, and the parents talked about what a pain he was, what a difficult kid he was, and how he'd flipped out the first time when he was twenty in the Army. When I picked him up, he was forty-three so he had been twenty years in and out of hospitals with his parents trying to help him. I started thinking, I even put a footnote on a paper about this, that this was not family therapy, it was a family examination. Because we hadn't thought of family therapy. It was only after I'd started a series of interviews to prepare them to take him home that everything changed in terms of thinking about schizophrenia as the product of a family and that something can be done to change it.

ELKAÏM: Tell me, Jay, you generally work behind the one-way mirror and you supervise people. When did you begin to work primarily in that way?

HALEY: The one-way mirror came into the field, I think, by a psychologist named Charles Fulweiler. He was over in Berkeley, in San Leandro in a juvenile home. He may be the earliest family therapist. He was seeing a teenage girl who had run away from home and been picked up in a bar out in the Valley. They brought her back and put her in the juvenile home and he tested her. He was a psychologist, testing and teaching testing. She came out with no neurotic problems on the testing, so he thought it was just some fluke and they discharged her. In a few weeks she was picked up drunk in some bar out in the Valley again, and she came back in. He tested her and she came out normal. Being a psychologist, he was puzzled over how this could be. He wondered, for some reason, what her home situation was like, and he brought her parents in. He had a one-way mirror room because he was watching students test patients. What he did was go behind the mirror and have the husband and wife come in the room with the daughter. They hadn't seen the daughter for six weeks, and they were so casual, and so cool.

The father said, "How are you?" and the mother said, "Can you get cigarettes in this place?" Fulweiler, who is a very intense guy, came out from behind the mirror. He went into the room and called the father out into the hall. He said, "Do you love your daughter?" The father said, "Of course," and Fulweiler said, "You go in there and tell her so." The father went in the room and Fulweiler went behind the mirror and watched. The father struggled and finally said to his daughter that he loved her. At that, the daughter started to cry, the mother started to cry, the father cried. They had a big emotional session. So Fulweiler asked them to come back next week and do it again. He began an arrangement, where he'd put a family in the room, he'd bring them out in the hall, talk to them, and send them back in again. Then he began to go in himself from behind the mirror.

ELKAÏM: When was that?

HALEY: I discovered him in 1957 and I think he said he was doing it from 1953 or 1954 on. When I heard about him, since we had never heard about family therapy anywhere else, I went over to watch him. I spent thirty sessions behind the mirror with him. I became so interested in that way of using the mirror. You could see and still stay out of it. When I went back, I suggested we put up a mirror, and we did. It's great for research to watch a family session. So we put in a one-way mirror, and then we got lots of visitors and they saw the one-way mirror and thought, "That's the way you do family therapy." With a one-way mirror! So that's where it came from as far as I know.

ELKAÏM: So when did you begin to see families behind the one-way mirror? In 1957?

HALEY: It must have been 1957. Perhaps 1956.

ELKAÏM: And, since then, do you see families as a therapist or mostly as a supervisor via your students?

HALEY: I went into practice in 1956 and was in practice for seven or eight years. I got out of it because I was doing research all day long and practice in the evenings and weekends. I was doing Ericksonian therapy, which was brief and a rapid turnover. In the daytime, we were seeing families of schizophrenics in the hospital, and I was at a private practice seeing them in the evening, so I saw them up until after the project ended. I almost stayed in it to make a living. One of the reasons I wanted to start *Family Process* [the first family therapy journal] was because it might make an income for me so I could drop practice. It never did make much income.

ELKAÏM: So in fact, from 1963 on, you began mostly to train people.

HALEY: No, in 1962, the project ended, and I went over to do some experimenting with families with the Mental Research Institute, which Jackson had just started. Jackson, by the way, had a tremendous influence on our project. So I went over to do some research and I wanted to be through with therapy. I wanted to be able to study families without thinking about how to change them. That's very hard once you've been into it. I couldn't see a family with an obese mother without thinking, "Well, I could do this and get her to lose weight this way" instead of just thinking, "This is a mother." But then what happened is that I wrote *Strategies of Psychotherapy*. While I was trying to study families and get away from therapy, that book began to produce people who wanted me to lecture and talk and discuss therapy, and so I got back into therapy again. Then I began to teach a brief therapy course at Palo Alto; that was a product of that book.

ELKAÏM: In what year did you begin to teach brief therapy courses?

HALEY: It must have been in 1963, when the book came out. Before that I taught classes in hypnotherapy and Erickson's brief therapy.

ELKAÏM: And did you start supervising people around that time?

HALEY: Oh, before that we were supervising people. In 1959, we got a grant from NIMH. We got two grants: One was to study family therapy, and John Weakland headed that one, and then we experimented with families, and I headed that one. So we divided at that point. That was 1959 or 1961.

ELKAÏM: When you think about the years you spent with Bateson, the years you went regularly to see Erickson, what are the first things that come to mind when you think about Bateson and Erickson?

HALEY: Erickson was a deviant in psychiatry, and Bateson was a deviant in anthropology. Neither one of them went along with their profession when they disagreed with it, so they tended to become isolates and were similar in that way. It meant that I was free to choose to think the way I pleased, because I didn't have to conform to a particular way. There was a real revolution in therapy at that time. Up until the 1950s, there were no directives in therapy. If you gave a directive, you were a cad, if you told somebody what to do at all. There was no behavior therapy, there was no family therapy. And one of the things that influenced me very much at that time is that I also met Alan Watts in 1953. That was a busy year! I took a course from him on Western psychiatry and Eastern philosophy with John Weakland and began to see that as a possible model for therapy. In Zen you have a master whose job it is to change somebody, and they don't do it with just conversation or exploring the past. They do it in a variety of ways. So that began to appear like an alternative to psychodynamic therapy at that time and entered into our project.

ELKAÏM: So in fact, you never published, together with Gregory Bateson, anything about all those years?

HALEY: We published many papers but not a book. We should have. We talked about it. By the end of the decade, ten years, we'd had enough of each other. I mean, we'd been together eight hours a day for ten years! And dealing with highly charged material, and controversial material, and a book. What happened was that Jackson, Watzlawick, and Beavin wrote *Pragmatics,* which summarized ideas from the project. It's not a good book, and Bateson didn't like it.

ELKAÏM: So tell me, why wasn't it a good book and why, according to you, didn't Bateson like it?

HALEY: Well, Bateson said to me, "What they did was take thirty of my ideas and they got them wrong." It was just enough incorrect so that you weren't quite in agreement with it. Watzlawick had never been in the project, and Jackson was not a theoretician. He was a clinician and very busy all the time. Actually, a research assistant largely wrote that book, Janet Beavin.

ELKAÏM: She wrote a part of the book?

HALEY: I think so. Watzlawick did quite a bit, too, because he writes well.

ELKAÏM: What you are basically saying is, "The ideas were there, but not in the way in which Bateson or myself would have expressed them." Still, that book played an incredibly important role in the field of family therapy, especially in Europe, for example, where for everyone, the systemic approach to therapy was through *Pragmatics.* Do you think it played a less important role here?

HALEY: Oh yes. It went into academia, but it didn't get out. There was no family therapy in academia. It was in private institutes. They needed a textbook of some kind and they used that one.

ELKAÏM: I remember one day you said at a conference in Brussels that one of the problems you had with the systemic approach to family therapy was the same problem you had with psychoanalysis: that in both situations, people explain why someone does something, but they don't try to change that person. You were defending some kind of strategic approach where the therapist would think about how to change the behavior, rather than just how to understand it. And this is a very important problem for many people in Europe, including Mara Selvini-Palazzoli today, because a lot of us are very interested in accepting that people come to see us to change, and they pay us to change.

HALEY: That was discovered in 1950.

ELKAÏM: But at the same time, we have a problem with intelligibility, with trying to understand why they behave that way. And for many of us, it doesn't seem that clear that understanding the thing from a different perspective will not lead to change. And for some of us, for example, there is not that clear-cut opposition between a systemic approach and an approach leading to change, if you can, for example, reframe what is happening in a way which prevents people from looking at it in the same way, and which opens up new avenues. But for you, it is more clear-cut.

HALEY: I think you can talk to everybody about their problems for years and they won't change unless you do something.

ELKAÏM: So, for example, reframing things in a way which makes people look at their predicament differently is not enough, you have to do something?

HALEY: There were two or three contributions to family therapy, and one was the idea that up to that time, your thoughts generated your behavior. If you wanted to change somebody, you changed the way they perceived and thought and so on. With family therapy, it was argued that your behavior organizes your thoughts and gives you ideas. Therefore if you want a person to have different ideas, you have to arrange a different social situation. That was a revolutionary idea, and very hard for intellectuals, because they've always felt that the proper understanding of man is man. If they could understand themselves, they'd be different.

ELKAÏM: But you see, Jay, in my own practice I often observed big changes after the first session. I didn't give a task, but I created a situation during the session in which I would reframe what was happening completely differently, and then we would see some change occur. Now we can perhaps call the fact that I created this situation which changed the way people relate to each other a 'task."

HALEY: But you know, there was also Bateson's classic statement that every message is a report and a command. And therefore, reframing is not just a report about how they should be different, it's a command to be different.

ELKAÏM: So in fact, what you're clearly saying is, a therapist has to accept that even when he's trying to simply reframe, to speak, he is in fact involved in giving a command, in doing something rather than just discussing.

HALEY: You can't not communicate.

ELKAÏM: You can't not also command in a way even if you don't want to.

HALEY: Let me just say another thing on that. You realize that you're going to communicate a command no matter what you do, then you notice things differently. Carl Rogers said he didn't give any directives, he just reflected back. If you watch him reflecting what a patient says, he chooses certain things to reflect; he doesn't reflect everything. So the patient begins to deliver more and more of those things.

ELKAÏM: Let's come back to that period. . . .

HALEY: One of the things that had an influence on me later was training people who were not educated to be therapists. It makes you realize how therapy was born in the university. Intellectuals love to think about themselves and to wonder why people do things, and explain things, instead of just taking some action to make a change. I think that once you train people who aren't intellectuals, you then look at the intellectuals in a different way.

ELKAÏM: Before we get to that and to the work you did with Sal Minuchin, I want to ask you for one more story. I remember once someone told me about something that happened to Don Jackson, and I want to check whether it was just a legend or if it really happened. Apparently, Don Jackson was told that there was a patient who thought he was a psychiatrist, and the other person was a psychiatrist who was told that he would see a patient who thought he was a psychiatrist. They then put Jackson and the other guy together. Did it really happen?

HALEY: Not like that.

ELKAÏM: Tell me the story.

HALEY: Bateson had trouble every time he tried to experiment. He couldn't do an experiment successfully perhaps because he was too much of an anthropologist. At any rate, he had this idea that schizophrenia was a confusion of communication about the relationship. Therefore, if you could set up a situation where two people had two different premises about what their relationship was, you might get schizophrenic behavior. He invited Jackson to see a patient at the VA. I think it's filmed; it's somewhere. It's one of the few times we filmed because it was so expensive. He set up Jackson to see this patient and he told the patient, "This other guy is going to come in; he's a patient who has the delusion that he's a psychiatrist. So he's going to talk to you like a psychiatrist and you should be patient with him, and we want to film this." So Jackson came in the room, and the patient came in the room, and they knew each other. They had met. Jackson didn't say anything, thinking, "Well maybe the guy flipped out and went in the hospital." The other guy thought, "Oh my God, maybe Jackson flipped out." But the whole thing went down the drain. What's interesting about the film is that Jackson turned him into a patient very skillfully, leading him on in such a way that pretty soon the guy was talking about his problems in the interview. But that was what happened. Every time Bateson set up an experiment like that, it went wrong.

ELKAÏM: I just want to see if I understood. There was a patient who was also a psychiatrist.

HALEY: I'm not sure he was even a patient, he was a guy anyhow, but he may have been a patient. I've forgotten.

ELKAÏM: And Bateson said to him, "You will meet someone who thinks he's a psychiatrist but who's not a psychiatrist." That was Jackson. And Jackson came in and in fact, what we know is that both of them received the information that the other one thought he was a psychiatrist, but they knew each other.

HALEY: It turned out they'd met, that's right.

ELKAÏM: And then it turned out that the guy became a patient with Don. It's an interesting story; it's like Columbus discovering America when he went looking for India. So Bateson began looking for something and found something else.

HALEY: Let me tell about another experiment that he did, that I don't think ever got written up. I'm sure it hasn't. We were interested in the idea that schizophrenics and their families talked like they'd just met each other. They didn't talk like they had confidence in their relationship. It was like they were getting acquainted. We wanted to experiment and the thought was that if we brought three strangers together of the appropriate ages, like the ages of parents and the age of a daughter, that when they got together and talked, we could show that to another group and say, "Is this a family of schizophrenics or not?" So it sounded like a very interesting idea and we got it all set up. We had this one-way mirrored room in Palo Alto where we were working, and we had a camera. Weldon Keyes was a poet who was our cameraman. We had the camera all set up, and we had these people in different rooms. They came together, and the man and woman sat down and began to talk. The man and woman were Caucasians and the daughter who came in was Filipino, which totally took out the idea that this was a family. The man was an anthropologist who had been to the Philippines, so he immediately started talking to her about the Philippines like two strangers would. So the whole experiment went down the drain. What Bateson had done is send over to the nurse's quarters a message that he'd like to have a nurse around eighteen or twenty years old for an interview and they sent over a Filipino.

ELKAÏM: This is some kind of curse, each time he does an experiment. . . !

HALEY: I was doing the family experimental program and Bateson was always saying to me, "Do an experiment; get an experiment!" I'd say, "Gregory I'll be happy to do whatever you can think of." Because we were into a new whole era of how to experiment with relationships, not with perception, and it was an interesting problem, but a really difficult one. We were trying to determine if family organizations were different. Was the family of a schizophrenic different from other families?

ELKAÏM: So you describe Gregory Bateson as someone who was trying to understand what was happening in reality. He was a discoverer, trying to find the patterns hidden behind things at different levels of functioning in life. He was someone who believed that there was something out there that we could find and use.

HALEY: Absolutely. He was a nineteenth-century philosopher in many ways. His father coined the term "genetics," you know; he was a biologist. And Bateson once said he'd never met a person without a master's degree until he was twenty-one. It was a very intellectual family, a sad one in some ways, but very intellectual.

ELKAÏM: So now the project is finished in Palo Alto; what happened then? What did you do? What year was it then?

HALEY: That was 1962. I went over to the MRI, the Mental Research Institute, with Jackson. Jackson, by the way, had written a paper on family homeostasis with systems. It came out in '57 and he said he wrote it in '53 or '54, so he'd written it a couple of years earlier. It took a long time to come out, like my 1958 paper took three years to come out. I was writing that when we were writing the double bind paper and I sent it to journals. They'd wait six months and they'd send it back, wanting some revision. I'd send it back, and it just went on and on. Anyhow, Jackson was very astute about relationships.

He was personally supervised by Sullivan, who used to make an issue about how the therapist was in the room as well as the patient and was influencing the patient by whatever he did—that was Sullivan's idea. He would always ask the therapist, "What were you doing when the patient did such and such?" The analysts in those days didn't like the idea that they were having any influence on the production of a patient. But anyhow, I was supervised by Jackson and that was his emphasis. What anybody in that family or any individual was doing was a product of what I was doing as well. I wasn't a neutral observer. He was one of the best clinicians I've ever seen. He was curing schizophrenics routinely with family therapy and he thought that wasn't much. He wanted to be a great researcher. He didn't want to be a clinician. It's a shame we didn't get more films of him at work. We only had some audiotapes. We thought he'd live forever, you know. But anyhow, he was a big influence. Then he arranged a grant for me. He was always hustling money to keep the Mental Research Institute going. There was an old church and he got me space in it. I began a whole series of communication experiments, comparing normal families to schizophrenic families, delinquent families, in tasks in which we were trying to get a measure. The question was, and it's still an obvious one, if schizophrenia is a product of the family, can you differentiate between a family with schizophrenics and another family on the basis of any kind of measurements? That's what I was struggling with then. I wrote about four or five papers on that and was beginning to get the hang of it. I spent five years experimenting and I had Alex Bavelas, a great social psychologist, as my consultant on experiments. It was an interesting time. What I had was an ongoing laboratory where I had a social worker whose job was just to bring in normal families, and they were hard to get in, teenagers particularly. Then I was trading talks at all the state hospitals around for abnormal families, and we made a portable testing thing to go test them. So that was the first experimenting with families really; I don't know if it's even being done anymore. Hopefully it got into the universities.

ELKAÏM: And then Sal Minuchin came to ask you to work with him. When was that?

HALEY: It must have been '66; '67 was when I went to work with him, so it must have been that year.

ELKAÏM: So for four or five years you were working at the MRI with Don Jackson?

HALEY: From '62 to '67 really.

ELKAÏM: What do you remember about those five years with him that was important to you?

HALEY: The idea of experimentation was the most important idea. If you have a husband and wife relating to each other, and another husband and wife relating to each other, how can you make a test that shows how they're similar or different? Not in their perception of each other, but the way they handle conflict, the way they reach agreement. It was an interesting task, and it still is. But that was the main thing. Also I was in practice for a good part of that time and still consulting with Erickson, who was in his own way supervising my work.

ELKAÏM: How was he supervising your work?

HALEY: Well, he did various things. I'd ask him about a case, and sometimes he would tell me something to do with it. More often, he would start talking about one of his own cases. But I'll give you an example; I was just writing a paper remembering this. I was seeing a couple, and the wife was very unhappy with the husband, who was kind of a passive guy. They both were.

On Saturday mornings she would vacuum the whole house, and he would come and walk behind her from room to room to room. He said this was a minor problem but it was driving her out of her mind. She couldn't stop her husband, and she'd say, "Don't follow me around the house." He would say, "Yes, dear" and then he would follow her around. So I said to Erickson, "What would you do with this?" and he said, "The answer's obvious," so I said, "Well, what is it?" and he said, "Tell the wife to vacuum the rooms and the husband will follow her. She's to go around to all the rooms where she vacuums, and she's to take the bag of dirt from the vacuum and dump a pile of dirt in each room. Then she's to say, 'Well, that's done,' and leave it there until the next Saturday. He won't follow her again." So I did it, and he didn't follow her. I asked him, "Why did that work?" He said, "People can't stand absurdity." That task is just too absurd. He can't take it so he'll go away from it.

ELKAÏM: That's interesting. So what you're saying to me is, "The way Erickson supervised me was to tell me, 'Be creative, find things which perhaps don't make sense, but which are very useful." Because absurdity in fact makes sense, the sense absurdity makes is that it gets away from what is expected. It stops repetition.

HALEY: Sure.

ELKAÏM: So, just one more thing: when did you write *Techniques of Family Therapy*? And when did you go to Philadelphia?

HALEY: 1967.

ELKAÏM: Can I ask you one thing? Why isn't Nathan Ackerman in that book?

HALEY: Well, I never thought of him as therapist. I thought of him as a family diagnostician. Also I was having trouble with him. There were also ideological differences that still continue. I have trained a number of the Ackerman Institute staff when they came to me, but I have never been invited to the Ackerman Institute. I have never been asked to lecture, give a seminar, or just visit. It's a different school from my approach to therapy, and it has been for thirty-five years.

ELKAÏM: I see. And you had the feeling that he was more a diagnostician than a therapist?

HALEY: If you asked him how you change somebody, he wouldn't have an answer. He would say, "Well, I get together with them, and I talk to them." He was a very skillful interviewer. I watched him interview, because I was watching therapists in those days. And he's got a nice film or two. I mean skillful in this sense: He saw a family with a crazy patient of some kind, and the guy had a brother in the room, and the brother said, "I think this whole thing is a waste of time." Ackerman turned to him and said, "I think you're very sharp about these things; I think you should be my co-therapist." Within seconds, this guy was disarmed and cooperating. That's what I mean by a skillful interviewer. He brought out the dynamics of families, but he also brought out all the negative stuff that psychodynamicists bring out, which made it very difficult to get the family to do something.

ELKAÏM: When you think back to that time in the '60s, who would you say were people who were important for the field of family therapy?

HALEY: When Jackson died, I organized an honorary meeting and brought in forty-five people from all over the country. That was about all the family therapists there were. Everybody who had any connection with the family, I brought to that meeting. It was at Asilomar in California. I've still got the audiotapes of that, and I've never published them or done anything with them. I was listening to one the other day to make sure it had something on it. But it would be interesting, because that's where everybody was fixed in ideas about 1968.

ELKAÏM: Tell me, what happened to Jackson at the end of his life?

HALEY: Well, a variety of things happened, I gather. He divorced his wife and took up with a girlfriend. I left about that time. That was a blow to him, because he and I were attached. I used to help him through some hard times. But he also started taking a variety of pills. He was found in a hotel room. He'd just got back from a workshop, and he died of an overdose of Pentathol. It looks like he was taking it to sleep, and sometimes you take it and forget you took it. I think that's what happened. Because I went back there, and spent a week talking to people about it and about the way he had his life organized. It didn't sound like he was going to withdraw and do himself in. He was so busy and had things so scheduled, and I'd been through some crises with him before and he never withdrew and got depressed. What he did was get more active, and busier and busier when he got upset. But he was a very busy fellow. I remember once counting twelve projects he was involved with, and those were only the ones I knew about. I mean, he was writing a book on the stock market with a guy; he was getting this kind of grant and that kind of grant; he was writing a book on cases; and he was hustling money to keep the place going.

ELKAÏM: But he wasn't sick?

HALEY: He wasn't sick, no.

ELKAÏM: And according to you, it was an accident.

HALEY: I think it could have been. At least it would be a mystery to me why he would kill himself. Even though he had a lot of troubles, it isn't the way he worked.

ELKAÏM: But was he having some trouble at the MRI at that time or not?

HALEY: He had trouble with everybody there probably, because he would get something started, and then he would pass it on to them and then he would get something else started. But he'd neglect what he passed on, because he'd expect others to take care of it. Often they didn't, they just got exasperated with him. And the place had no money; it was really a way of people using private practice to make a living and getting research grants on the side. He couldn't get enough money for the place to make it a research endeavor, really, so he had to settle for whoever would come. It was a hard time getting it going.

ELKAÏM: So at that time, at the MRI, who was there?

HALEY: There was Jules Riskin and John Weakland. After the Bateson grant ended, John went away for a year or so, and then he came to the MRI, so he was there. Watzlawick was there; Virginia Satir was in and out of there.

ELKAÏM: How was your relationship with Satir?

HALEY: I enjoyed her. She was a formidable woman. A couple of things about her. She wanted to be a great theoretician, and she was not a theoretician. One day she said to John and Gregory and I that she had it all solved, theoretically, the whole family issue. She would like us to come and listen to her. She had a room with a big blackboard at the MRI, so we came over and we listened. It was absolute balderdash! I can't even remember what she said. Bateson said, "Well, that's interesting," and he left, and John left. Virginia said something to me like, "I don't know why they didn't appreciate this." I said, "Virginia, it isn't what you thought it was, it's really just not good—it's awful." She put her face right up in front of mine and she said, "Jay, I don't understand your love messages"! She was a great publicist for family therapy. We went on the road and talked about family therapy and people found it interesting. When she went around, they started doing it. She turned on people all over the country to family therapy. She probably had more influence than anybody else. Then she was on the road all the time. She once told me she was in the air 300 days a year, or something like that, toward the end.

ELKAÏM: Let's talk about the moment when Sal Minuchin came to Palo Alto to see you and invite you to work with him. How was it?

HALEY: Well, an unusual thing happened with it. He called and said he wanted to see me, and I said, "Well, why don't you stay at my house?" He said "Okay." I had never invited any visitors to stay at my house. He just appealed to me in some way. What he came for was to offer me a job. I didn't know he was going to do that; I just thought he was visiting. He used to travel around watching people, too. I had seen him at Wiltwyck in New York and I'd been behind the mirror there with him and Braulio Montalvo. There was an interesting difference there between us. They had a mother, two kids, and a grandmother, black kids, delinquent kids, and they were bringing them behind the mirror, and taking them back in the room. They were interpreting to the boys about their mother, and about their relationship with their grandmother, and so on. The mother was an attractive lady but she had no front teeth. She talked with her hand covering the gap in her teeth and was a very shy woman. They were doing a kind of interpretative structural therapy, and when the session ended, they asked me what I would do with that family. I said I would ask the boys to earn money to get a bridge for their mother's front teeth. They should raise the money to do that. They shouldn't steal it. That should be their project, because their mother would be a lot happier having her front teeth. The therapist thought that was crazy that I was neglecting the whole family structure and what was happening with these delinquent kids. But I'm sure those kids would have done it, and I don't think they would have stolen to do it. It's strictly an Ericksonian thing, and that's what I pointed out. This is what Erickson would do; he'd pick the issue, an issue, like the front teeth, and organize the whole family around changing that. So anyhow, I enjoyed Minuchin and Braulio. When Sal came out and hired me, Palo Alto didn't have any poor. It had a little token slum near it, really. The whole world was changing in the '60s. The poor were everywhere, and there were demonstrations and so on. I had the chance to get a salary and go to Philadelphia where there were plenty of poor. I took that opportunity. Also I was living from grant to grant and raising kids on it and it was getting harder and harder. I needed a salary and Sal promised me that I could come there, get a salary, and not have to do anything I didn't want to. So that was great. The first couple of years, I did whatever I wanted. I did research with kids there and so on. Finally Sal said, "You know, you have to do something," and I began to teach there.

ELKAÏM: It's interesting, because in fact Sal did with you what Gregory Bateson did with you.

HALEY: Leave me free, yes.

ELKAÏM: Both of them, and you chose what you enjoyed.

HALEY: I had ten years of that with Bateson, to do whatever I wanted.

ELKAÏM: So how long did you remain with Sal Minuchin in Philadelphia?

HALEY: It was nine years, I think, ten years.

ELKAÏM: Can you tell me a little about those years?

HALEY: Well, there were extraordinary changes. When I went there, Sal had just taken over the Child Guidance Clinic and actually, he didn't have his medical degree. He had a foreign one, Argentinean, and it wasn't accepted in the States. He couldn't run this clinic unless he got it and he said he wasn't about to go study and take a test. They were so eager to get him that the legislature passed an honorary degree or whatever, so that he could practice. He took over that clinic. It was a clinic in a black neighborhood, because it was the maid's neighborhood, and it drew all the rich people from the suburbs to the clinic, not the local people at all, not the neighborhood. He turned it into a neighborhood clinic with a family orientation and he lost 95 percent of his staff. They just left.

ELKAÏM: Why did they leave?

HALEY: They couldn't tolerate the changes. They didn't know how to work with families, and they didn't really want to work with families. They were against the whole idea, just like child psychiatry places are today. But Sal looks on it as a positive thing. He says it gave him a chance to get new people. That's why he went and got me, because he needed somebody connected with families, and he was lonely, too. When I got there, there were twelve people on the staff and they sat around the table and talked about a case. When I left, nine years later, there were three hundred, and there were two satellite clinics besides the big clinic, which moved on to the campus. So he made tremendous changes, and he did the same thing Jackson did. He would start a project and then he would pass it to somebody else and start another one. And that's how he kept that place financed. He usually passed them to Braulio, and Braulio had to finish them, and fortunately he did.

ELKAÏM: My dear Jay, let's talk about the work you were doing with Sal. When you came to Wiltwyck, he was surprised to see you propose an idea which was an Ericksonian idea about the bridge for the mother. How did you succeed in connecting his structural approach with your strategic one? At that time, you were a strategician already, and you had written a book on strategic psychotherapy, so how did you connect that together at the time?

HALEY: Well, I didn't. The first couple of years, I filmed young people—young blacks, young whites—doing different things. I was interested in the research idea that you teach people how to use a camera, and then you let them shoot whatever they want. You see how they see the world. Some interesting stuff came out of those kids. For example, the black kids filmed each other dancing, or fighting, or stealing, or whatever. The middle-class blacks and whites filmed the corner of a building, or a tree, or a house. No people were in their films at all. That was independent of race; it was a middle class/poor distinction. The poor whites danced and filmed themselves dancing. I was interested in that sort of thing, and I was trying to film relationships and the rules for them. Then I had to begin to teach, because Sal was getting more staff that had to be taught, and he wanted me to earn my money more, so I began to teach. I realized quickly that I couldn't teach an Ericksonian approach in that setting, partly because of Sal.

He didn't like anything paradoxical or anything manipulative, or anything indirect really, and he would go along with it, but reluctantly. The problem was, there were guys applying for child psychiatry to train with me who wanted that. So I would do things on the side with them, but the main bulk of the teaching I would do was a structural kind of family therapy. Then I started a sample of schizophrenics; we had no schizophrenics in the clinic because the age limit was 18 and most of them are older. So I did it in the evenings, I did twenty-five cases or something like that, with anybody who would bring in their family. But I did things on the side really, while the central stuff, I did pretty well what Sal and Braulio would do. Braulio was interested in Erickson, learned hypnosis, and was more flexible.

TRAINING THE POOR

Jay Haley and Braulio Montalvo spent almost ten years at the Philadelphia Child Guidance Clinic together with Salvador Minuchin, innovating training of local community people to work in mental health. This is an excerpt from an interview by Madeleine Richeport-Haley as they reminisced about those years. Margarita Montalvo was also present.

RICHEPORT-HALEY: How did you meet?

MONTALVO: I went to look for you in Palo Alto. You were in a church basement. I was pretty impressed. You had data all over the walls of Orientals who had just come off the boat.

HALEY: I was studying the Japanese. I was getting into abstract sequences.

MONTALVO: Jay had just finished writing *Strategies of Psychotherapy* and Sal sent me to check you out. He wanted to bring you back east.

HALEY: I came to visit you in New York. It was after *Family Process* started, because I would go anywhere there was a family being seen to get a paper.

MONTALVO: You were over the whole map.

HALEY: I began to have that function. I began to be the only one who knew who was seeing families. I remember Ray Birdwhistell who would not publish until he got it perfect. I remember going up to him and taking the paper out of his hand.

RICHEPORT-HALEY: Can you describe the program?

MONTALVO: We were interviewing high school graduates and giving them patients to cure. We had to train them as therapists interviewing them and deciding whether they should have 100,000 dollars invested in them. It was hard to guess. We never interviewed people before who had no academic background. We always checked if they had a PhD, as if that was relevant.

HALEY: I remember one of those you interviewed—you asked him, "Suppose you had a boy who wets the bed. And his brother has a motorcycle that has a gas leaking out. What would you do with this problem?" I thought this was a great way to deal with metaphor.

MONTALVO: The amazing thing was how many of them went right to it. I remember I talked to Paul through pool.

HALEY: This was Paul Riley. He was a pool shark.

RICHEPORT-HALEY: Who was Paul Riley? Did you train him?

MONTALVO: He was a man from the community without any formal mental health training and some of them became excellent counselors.

HALEY: He was one of the best therapists I've known.

MONTALVO: They were not mistrained.

HALEY: They were not taught what they had to unlearn. I remember I started the first day. There were eight or ten and I talked to them about therapy and told them what I knew. The next day they came in and I had to talk to them about therapy for eight hours. On the third and fourth day I did it some more. I didn't have a fifth day. I was ready to start giving them families. In other seminars you give them a book to read and a film to see. We just put them in with families.

MONTALVO: Empirical training—they proceeded from true interactive questions and dilemmas. It was more heavy-duty frontline apprenticeship than anything I've seen.

HALEY: We put them in with families within two weeks. Eight hours a day seeing families steadily and being helped and protecting the families by supervision behind the mirror.

MONTALVO: They also had to write reports and many of them were having a tough time with English. I remember we hired teachers.

HALEY: I don't know if you remember this. I got interested in having mothers of schizophrenics treat mothers of schizophrenics because we had some successful cases. Those women could treat someone with the same problem. I could never get it organized having mothers who had been through therapy work with these poor mothers in helping them to be good parents. It was a very similar idea. Somehow Sal got a grant, not to deal with the mothers, but to get high school graduates and train them to treat families.

MONTALVO: To use the poor to help the poor. Of all the programs teaching the poor, this is the one they stayed in.

HALEY: We taught them to do therapy. We did not teach them to teach. Then they were asked by the staff to teach and they didn't know how. It made me realize for the first time the difference between teaching and therapy. They had some remarkable results. One of them went to get a job in a poor agency. She had a husband who drank and eight kids. She left him during the program. In the program, she got a reputation pretty fast of being competent. I remember she came to me with a family of a schizophrenic and she came to Sal with an anorectic. They kept being asked to do more than they were trained to do.

MONTALVO: It's really amazing. I don't think they do that with a doctor, asking him to deal with anything. Ninety percent kept jobs in mental health.

HALEY: We also tried to get them GEDs and master's degrees. One of them got an MA. It was hard for a place to hire them because the job was based on a degree and they didn't have degrees.

Black militants began to oppose the program, saying that you are training second-class citizens for second-class people. We invited them over to watch a case. They saw a black person treating a white family. They went away and never came again.

MONTALVO: I also struggled with that when an upper-middle-class family found themselves with a therapist who said "ain't."

HALEY: I did a study of 200 families in the clinic to see if these therapists did as well as the staff. I did a simple thing, asking them when they came in, "What is the problem?" and when they finished, "Are they over the problem?" In fact, the poor people did better than the staff. But the staff wasn't supervised or trained that well. One of the therapists came down the hall and said, "I just got a twelve-year-old boy out of his mother's bed." I said, "What did you do?" He said, "Well, I talked to the mother and said, 'You know your son as he gets older, he's going to have erections and if he's in bed with you he's going to feel very embarrassed. To save him that embarrassment, can you find him a bed of his own?' She said, 'Sure.' And she did that. She didn't feel guilty. She was not blamed. It was so smoothly done.

MONTALVO: Looking through the mirror and looking at that skill in that dialogue.

HALEY: It was so nice to have something to look forward to that was of interest. Every day was interesting. What I see myself doing more and more is introducing common sense and think you are, too. I was watching someone talking about depression who said, "People get depressed because they are in depressing situations." And I think that's what family therapy introduced.

MONTALVO: Respecting contemporary contexts.

ELKAÏM: Today a lot of people would see work that is at the same time structural, paradoxical, and strategic as completely coherent, because they would say that sometimes it's easier to give paradoxical tasks than to give straightforward tasks that people won't do. And some people will try to use your two approaches, the structural one and the strategic one, at the same time without seeing any opposition. But at that time it wasn't that easy?

HALEY: No, well, it still isn't. I've been writing a book on supervision and looking at what's happening. Supervisors are still the way they were, trained in psychodynamic, nondirective approaches, and they've got students out in the field who are telling people what to do and don't know how to do that.

ELKAÏM: So tell me, at that time you were training paraprofessionals, people from the street, people who hadn't finished high school, I suppose.

HALEY: No, they'd finished high school. It wasn't quite like that. Here's what happened: I got interested in the idea of a mother of a schizophrenic treating another family with a schizophrenic, because they were so sharp and they were experienced. I thought, "If I can cure a family with a schizophrenic, I'll ask the mother to cure another one." Sal was interested in working with the poor, getting the mothers to change the way they dealt with the kids, and then having those mothers change other mothers. So we came together talking about this idea. The original idea was to train mothers, or fathers, but they were mostly mothers. Sal applied for a grant and in the process of making it a grant, it became people who were poor to treat the poor, rather than people who were experienced in therapy as patients. So we then began to interview people and it was an interesting problem. We were going to train them forty hours a week for a year or two years. So it meant putting 100,000 dollars into this person. You had to decide whether it was a person you wanted to train that much. So we interviewed a whole stack of people. The women were easy; they were very competent women. The men, if they would settle for the stipend we could offer, they hadn't succeeded much in life and they were pretty unsuccessful guys. Also, we had women who would bring their husbands in and say, "Here's one," and he would say, "Where am I?" But we required, as I remember, that they have a high school education.

ELKAÏM: And did you enjoy that work?

HALEY: Oh, I enjoyed it immensely. I think that may be where live supervision really came in. In Palo Alto, I had done supervision with people with schizophrenic families, staying behind the mirror and watching them, and then talking about the session afterwards. But we didn't intrude; we didn't knock on the door, or call in. Then in the next step, we began to knock on the door and to bring them out, and influence them during the session, which was a remarkable idea. When we got to the poor, we had to protect the families from total novices, and therefore we used live supervision very much. We planned the session with them, we put them in there, we called them on the phone, we called them out, we coached them, we sent them back, and it was a very hands-on supervision. The teaching was a task. We had a group of ten or fifteen, and the first day, we had them for eight hours and I taught for eight hours. The next day, we had them for eight hours and I taught for eight hours. The third day, I'd taught everything I knew, and that's why we put them in with families pretty fast! Always before, we trained people for a couple of hours or half a day.

ELKAÏM: At that time, I was working in Bronx State Hospital and I was training paraprofessionals. I was directing a mental health center in the South Bronx, called the Mott Haven Mental Health Center, and we created something called the Lincoln Family Therapy Training Program, where we were training paraprofessionals. In '75, I organized a meeting in New York which you took part in with two of your students for a couple of hours, or half a day with your students, with Marianne Walters. Do you remember? It was on the grounds of the Bronx State Hospital. Chris Beels was there, and Al Scheflen. You were so kind. We didn't have any money, and we were very egalitarian, so we paid the students, your paraprofessionals, Marianne Walters, and yourself the same amount, and you were so generous. I remember how our students were very much interested by what you were saying then, because it made sense for all of them. In fact, the training we were doing in Lincoln was a little different from what you were doing, because you were really giving them tools, very clear tools, while we were trying to help them find their own way toward solving some difficult situations, which was not easy, because not everyone has the creativity or the intuition to be able to create something new in a situation like that. So in fact, a lot of them will fall back on your tools each time they get stuck, using the structural approach or the strategic approach. You didn't call that strategic at the time.

HALEY: I don't know what it was called, but one of the things I did in *Problem-Solving Therapy* was write a chapter on how to do a first interview with families, and it came out of that work, because they needed to know, "How do I sit?" and "Where do I stand?" and "What if the kid's over here?" That has turned out to be very helpful for a lot of people, just doing a competent interview.

ELKAÏM: Yes, I remember that chapter very well, which gave step-by-step advice: You speak with them, and then you do this and that. It was very helpful. So for you, these years were an important time. You at least had a salary from year to year; you didn't have to look for a grant at the end of each year, and you were writing at the time.

HALEY: Oh, I was writing at the time, yes. I was finishing up *Uncommon Therapy* then.

ELKAÏM: And you began *Ordeal Therapy* at that time also?

HALEY: I think so, yes.

ELKAÏM: And what happened then? You worked with Sal for nine years, then Sal stopped, and you stopped. Why?

HALEY: I stopped just before Sal did. Well, the place was getting so big and I was getting more interested in doing my own kind of therapy and my own kind of training really. I think I began to think I'd like to have my own institute so I could do it my own way.

ELKAÏM: So when you left, Sal left also.

HALEY: I think he probably did. It was just so big; I mean, 300 people and an inpatient unit, a school, and you're into the confusion. I tried to get Sal to keep the old building and just have training there and let everybody else go with the new building, and he couldn't do it. They were supposed to have to sell that in order to pay for the new one. But I just drove by the old one and it's sitting there with the windows caved in, trees growing out of the front door; it's just an abandoned building. It was an extraordinary building, with one-way mirrored rooms. It was very nice.

ELKAÏM: So then you came to Chevy Chase.

HALEY: What we did was get a room down at 3000 Connecticut Avenue. We started with me giving courses that people came to, and who would then register for more training. Actually, the first group of trainees, there were about eight or ten of them, all became our supervisors later. It was an interesting first group.

So then we moved to Chevy Chase where we got a house and had three floors, and that got so busy. We had a state grant to train everybody in Maryland. We would have three families going at once, and run up and down stairs, and we had eight to ten supervisors; it was so busy. You know, I went over and visited Milan, and they had it so leisurely. They had one case that they'd talk about in the morning and then discuss for a couple of hours, and then go to lunch and come back and talk about it in the afternoon. Then I decided it was crazy of me to run up and down stairs with three cases at my own training institute, so we slowed down a great deal at that point.

ELKAÏM: And now, are you still working at the Institute?

HALEY: No, I left the Institute several years ago.

ELKAÏM: And what do you do now?

HALEY: I just do workshops, a little supervision. I'm not sure what I'm going to do yet.

ELKAÏM: So how do you feel now at this moment in your life?

RICHEPORT-HALEY: Tell him about following Bateson's interest in Bali—you became interested yourself.

HALEY: We went over to Bali and spent four months there. We were making a film on Balinese children dancers.

ELKAÏM: When did you go there?

RICHEPORT-HALEY: We've been there more than once; the last time was about a year-and-a-half ago.

HALEY: We went to the village where Bateson and Mead spent their time and filmed some there, so that was interesting. But anyhow, I'm sort of looking for a purpose now. I'm writing a book on supervision, to be called *Learning and Teaching Therapy*, and I do a workshop every couple of months, just to make a living, really.

ELKAÏM: Tell me, what do you think about all of this constructivist movement, or constructionist movement?

HALEY: I think it's back to the individual. It's an emphasis on how the person constructs reality, or perceives reality, or thinks about reality. There's no dyad in it.

ELKAÏM: So for you, there's a move back to individual therapy?

HALEY: There's an inertia that takes people back to the individual again and again and again. There's some reluctance to move. I think it's the supervisors holding up the field from becoming more of a social orientation. I mean, right now, it's a curious situation: we have 180 ethnic groups coming in, we have every kind of psychopathology there is, we have all the court-ordered cases with abusive sex, and physical, and all kinds, and therapists are thrown in with these problems, and they don't know what to do. They turn to the supervisor, and the supervisor is teaching the way they taught twenty years ago, the way their teachers taught them. So they say, "I wonder why this is so upsetting to you?" If the person says, "I have this guy who never takes a bath. How can I get him to take a bath?" the supervisor will say, "I wonder why you're concerned about that. Is there something about bathing that's personally important to you?" That is, they don't say, "There's three ways to get this guy to take a bath, you know, and you could try any one of these," which is what I think the field needs more of, and has been developing for several years, but the supervisors aren't there.

ELKAÏM: You see, my own point of view is perhaps a little different, because at the same time, I am very close to you on the subject of doing concrete things, for example, if someone doesn't take a bath. But at the same time, I don't think there is an opposition between the idea of being effective in psychotherapy while at the same time taking an interest in the feelings of the therapist; on the contrary. Do you remember one day you spoke about a child who was putting things in his anus, and you spoke about how you gave a task to have a hole in the back yard and you gave three interpretations of the task. You said it was a structural task because it made the father come closer to the

child. It was ordeal therapy, because the ground was quite difficult to dig; it was autumn and it was quite cold. At the same
time, you said it was a metaphorical task. When you were
speaking about that task, someone in the audience said, "Why
so many feet by so many feet?" and you said that once when you
were in the army, when someone was smoking, he was told,
"Make a hole so many feet by so many feet and put your cigarettes in it." Do you remember? So for me, the task is more than
just the task. It is the task you give to them in that situation.
What do you think is interesting to say to readers who are family therapists working today in the field? What would you like
to say to them about their field?

HALEY: I think it's better not to call yourself a family therapist; it's
better to be a therapist who takes the family into account. If you
say you're a family therapist, then you have to do it a certain
way, and there are wrong ways. You can deviate from the proper
family therapy, so you're into arguments like, "Can you see an
individual if you're seeing families?" and all those crazy things
that happen with rules. But I think there is a tremendous inertia
to go back, as well as financial reasons for doing an individual,
long-term therapy. But what's happening in this country now is
managed care deciding how long therapy will be and who will
do it. People who don't know anything about therapy are making major decisions on how much to pay for it, and how long,
what you can do, and what you can't do.

ELKAÏM: Jay, I remember one day, I think it was at the end of the
'70s, we met in Zurich. At the time you associated me with
those people who were contesting; at the time I was coordinat-
ing a network for alternatives to psychiatry, and you told me,
"Mony, the fact that I ally with the parents, that I give power to
the parents to help the child, do you see that as reactionary?"
and I was surprised, because for me you were a very progressive
person. I always saw you as someone who gave a lot of energy,
of creativity, to work in poor neighborhoods, to create tools for

poor people, to create tools for, in fact, people who didn't have the academic knowledge of someone like Gregory Bateson. I was very touched that you could feel that some people would see you as taking the side of, I don't know, some kind of establishment because you were allying with the parents.

HALEY: Young people tend to think that, young therapists. You know, one of the things we did in the '50s when we got into family therapy was to start wrong. We joined the patient against the parents. Bateson particularly attacked parents and was saving these patients from them, but all of us did that. We also made interpretations and pointed things out to people that just upset them. It took a long while to get turned around to thinking in terms of hierarchy, and to thinking in terms of a more positive way of guiding them so they preferred to go with you.

ELKAÏM: That's why I felt your article of '58 was so crucial, in which you described the mother who says to the child, "Come sit on my lap," and then becomes rigid, and the child feels the double bind. The child will come and say to the mother, "Oh Mother, what a beautiful necklace you have" or "What beautiful earrings you have" so that the mother doesn't know if she's coming for the earrings or for her. When you wrote that in '58, it was very important for us, because it went beyond a situation in which someone traps someone else, and opened up a new way of looking at things where it's no longer a question of who's right and who's wrong, but "What is it that they are doing together?" Then, even if you ally with the parents, you are allying with the parents in a context where you don't ally with the strong against the weak, but you are trying to see where to put the lever to move the rock which is blocking the way.

ELKAÏM: And I also remember your beautiful tape with that guy whose daughter was breaking framed pictures and using the broken glass to attack her parents. I remember that you had them listen to children's songs on a Fisher Price record player and dance together. What I really loved about that kind of task is the fact that there isn't only the absurdity; it opens everything up and there is freedom, there is fresh air. What I also liked is that you can be very ethical and at the same time give a task which helps people who are caught in the same repetitive patterns to see things and live things completely differently. The importance of ethics makes me accept the point of view of my feminist friends that we did family therapy as if men and women were interchangeable.

HALEY: That record-playing technique was actually cited by Neil Schiff. Well, you know, there's another aspect to men and women. Feminists, I think, underestimate the power of women. The man may have the money and he may have community support and so on, but the wife has a whole range of things she can do, including having symptoms, that incapacitate a man. I mean, they're well-matched in many ways.

ELKAÏM: This is your theory from *The Power Tactics of Jesus Christ,* that there are different kinds of power. In fact, I always saw psychotherapy as a way to open people up to new situations, to give individuals more freedom—as an approach where psychotherapists are not tools of social control, but persons trying to free people. And that's why for me it's important, while refraining from imposing our point of view on the clients, to take into account the relationship of power which exists in society.

HALEY: You can't separate who you're an agent of. I mean, we used to be an agent of the individual, and then we were the agent of families, and now we're the agent of the state, with court-ordered cases, but it's a question of whether you're the agent of the wife or the agent of the husband if you think that way, too.

ELKAÏM: Or you can think that you're an agent of change in that situation and that you are working for both of them.

HALEY: That's right, if you can think in terms of all of them.

ELKAÏM: Thank you very much, my dear Jay. Do you have some last wise things you'd like to say?

HALEY: Words of wisdom? You know, I think there's been progress from the individual of the '50s, to the dyad of the '60s, and best represented by Erickson, to a triad where you think in terms of coalitions. I think it's very hard to blend those units. The constructivists are not noticing who they're joining in the family against whom when they're focused on perception and how people perceive the world. There's another thing about Europe that interests me. I think so much of Erickson, and so much of theory in the States, is rural. It comes from the American Middle West really. That is, you would never hear Erickson quoting Rousseau or a European intellectual; he would talk about life on the farm and what happened with the animals. European therapists don't seem to talk about how to get a cow into the barn.

ELKAÏM: I told you I had the impression that, as therapists, we use whatever we have, and I learned a lot from Ray Bradbury, who wrote *Martian Chronicles,* or Kafka, or Borges, and they are part of my life and part of my work. Kafka was someone who spoke about the absurdity of life, and how we can survive in a world. . .

HALEY: . . . that is just absurd.

ELKAÏM: And Erickson would say, "Then use it! Accept the absurdity!"

HALEY: Well, I never heard Erickson mention Kafka, but he thought that way. He certainly talked about absurdity.

HALEY: There's no digital information in the unconscious; it's all metaphor really.

ELKAÏM: It's also something I like in your work—the importance of the symptom as a metaphor.

HALEY: Oh sure.

ELKAÏM: And that for me is very important, because speaking of the symptom as a metaphor is accepting that there is intelligibility to the symptom, even if we know that explaining could be useless. T. S. Eliot said a very interesting thing one day. He once asked what was important in poetry? What is the meaning of the poem? If it was that important, you would not write poetry; you would write prose.

HALEY: That's true.

ELKAÏM: Still, you give some meaning to the poem, even if you know that what is important in poetry is the rhythm, the music. And Erickson, with his metaphorical tasks and his stories, tried to speak directly to the unconscious in its own language. I think that work which uses metaphors respects the intelligibility of what's happening, while trying to achieve change. Change, like symptoms, appears in a context which makes sense.

HALEY: It's also the consequences of change, and how to deal with the relapse—the expectation that this is a sequence, it isn't an intervention.

ELKAÏM: That is also something I learned from you: the notion of sequences. That people don't go from sickness to health, that there are sequences, there are different moments and you have to accept to go through them.

HALEY: That's true.

ELKAÏM: Thank you so much, my dear Jay.

Appendix B

Bibliography of Works by Jay Haley

BOOKS AND ARTICLES

1940s

(1947, 5 July). The eastern question. *The New Yorker,* 23, 53.

1950s

(1952). The appeal of the moving picture. *Quarterly of Film, Radio and Television,* 4, 361-374.

(1952, September). Charlie and fire extinguisher. *Bluebook Adventure in Fact and Fiction,* 96-100.

(1954, June). The great snafu. *Cavalier for Men,* 30-36.

(1955). Paradoxes in play, fantasy and psychotherapy. *Psychiatric Research Reports,* 2, 52-58.

(1956). Toward a theory of schizophrenia. *Behavioral Science,* *1*(25), 251-264. With G. Bateson, D. Jackson, and J. Weakland.

(1958). The art of psychoanalysis. *ETC.,* 15, 190-200.

(1958). An international explanation of hypnosis. *American Journal of Clinical Hypnosis,* 1, 41-57.

(1959). Control in psychoanalytic psychotherapy. *Progress in Psychotherapy,* 4, 48-65.

(1959). The family of the schizophrenic: A model system. *American Journal of Nervous and Mental Disease,* 129, 357-374.

Directive Family Therapy
Published by The Haworth Press, Inc., 2007. All rights reserved.
doi:10.1300/5883_11

(1959). An international description of schizophrenia. *Psychiatry,* 22, 321-332.

(1959). A transcript of trance induction with commentary. *American Journal of Clinical Hypnosis, 2,* 39-84. With J. Weakland.

1960s

(1960). Control of fear with hypnosis. *American Journal of Clinical Hypnosis, 2,* 109-115.

(1960). Observation of the family of the schizophrenic. *American Journal of Orthopsychiatry, 30,* 466-467.

(1961). Control in brief psychotherapy. *Archives of General Psychiatry, 4,* 139-153.

(1961). Control in the psychotherapy of schizophrenics. *Archives of General Psychiatry, 5,* 340-353.

(1962). Family experiments: A new type of experimentation. *Family Process, 12,* 265-293.

(1962). Whither family therapy? *Family Process, 1,* 69-100.

(1963). Marriage therapy. *Archives of General Psychiatry, 8,* 213-234.

(1963, March). A note on the double bind. *Family Process, 2*(1).

(1963). *Strategies of psychotherapy.* New York: Grune & Stratton.

(1963). Transference revisited. *Journal of Nervous and Mental Disease, 137,* 363-372. With Don D. Jackson.

(1964). Research on family patterns: An instrument measurement. *Family Process, 3,* 41-65.

(1965). The art of being schizophrenic. *Voices, 1,* 133, 142.

(1965). Szasz: Law, liberty and psychiatry: An inquiry into the social uses of mental health practices. *California Law Review, 53,* 2.

(1967). Cross-cultural experimentation: An initial attempt. *Human Organization, 3,* 110-117.

(1967). The doctor as part of the schizophrenic interchange. *International Journal of Psychiatry, 4*(6), 534-542.

(1967). Experiment with abnormal families. *Archives of General Psychiatry*, 53-63.

(1967). An ordeal for pleasure, a story. *Voices, 3,* 109-118.

(1967). The perverse triangle. In J. Zuk & I. Nagy (Eds.), *Family therapy and disturbed families.* Palo Alto, CA: Science and Behavior Books.

(1967). Speech sequences of normal and abnormal families with two children present. *Family Process, 1,* 81-97.

(1967). *Techniques of family therapy.* New York: Basic Books. With Lynn Hoffman.

(1968). *Advanced techniques of hypnosis and therapy: Selected papers of Milton H. Erickson.* New York: Grune & Stratton.

(1968). The amiable hippie. *Voices, 4,* 102-110.

(1968). Testing parental instructions of schizophrenic and normal children: A pilot study. *Journal of Abnormal Psychology, 73,* 559-565.

(1969). The art of being a failure as a therapist. *American Journal of Orthopsychiatry, 39,* 691-695.

(1969). *The power tactics of Jesus Christ and other essays.* New York: Grossman.

1970s

(1970). Approaches to family therapy. *International Journal of Psychiatry, 9,* 233-242.

(1970). How to criticize your fellow therapist. *Voices, 6,* 16-20.

(1971). *Changing families: A family therapy reader.* New York: Grune & Stratton.

(1971). Communication and therapy: Blocking metaphors. *American Journal of Psychotherapy, 25,* 214-227.

(1971). Family therapy: A radical change. In J. Haley (Ed.), *Changing families: A family therapy reader* (pp. 272-284). New York: Grune & Stratton.

(1971). Reaction to socio-documentary film research in a mental health clinic. *American Journal of Orthopsychiatry, 4,* 91-100. With R. Chalfen.

(1972). Critical overview of present status of family interaction research. In J. L. Framo (Ed.), *Family interaction* (pp. 13-49). New York: Springer.

(1972). Family therapy and research: An annotated bibliography of articles and books published 1950-1970. New York: Grune & Stratton. With Ira D. Glick.

(1972). Fourteen ways to fail as a teacher of family therapy. *Family Therapy, 1,* 1-8.

(1973). In defense of child therapy. *Family Process, 12,* 227-244. With B. Montalvo.

(1973). Strategic therapy when a child is presented as a problem. *Journal of the American Academy of Child Psychiatry, 12,* 641-659.

(1973). *Uncommon therapy: The psychiatric techniques of Milton H. Erickson, M.D.* New York: W. W. Norton.

(1975). Familientherapie mit gestorten jugendlichen. *Zentralblatt &r EHEund Familienkunde, 3,* 148-161.

(1975). Family therapy. In A. M. Freedman, H. I. Kaplan, & B. J. Sadock (Eds.), *Comprehensive textbook of psychiatry* (2nd ed., pp. 1881-1885). Baltimore: Williams and Wilkins.

(1975). Why a mental health clinic should avoid family therapy. *Journal of Marriage and Family Counseling, 1,* 3-13.

(1976). Development of a theory: A history of a research project. In C. Sluzki (Ed.), *The double bind.* New York: Norton.

(1976). *Problem-solving therapy: New strategies for effective family therapy.* San Francisco: Jossey-Bass.

(1977). Dimensions of family therapy. *Journal of Nervous and Mental Disease, 165*(2), 88-98. With C. S. Madanes.

(1977). A quiz for young therapists. *Psychotherapy, 14,* 165-168.

1980s

(1980). How to be a marriage therapist without knowing practically anything. *Journal of Marriage and Family Therapy, 6*(4), 385-392.

(1980). *Leaving home: The therapy of disturbed young people.* New York: McGraw-Hill.

(1981). *Reflections on therapy and other essays.* Washington, DC: Family Therapy Institute.

(1982). The contribution to therapy of Milton H. Erickson. In J. K. Zeig (Ed.), *Ericksonian approaches to hypnosis and psychotherapy.* New York: Brunner-Mazel.

(1984). *Ordeal therapy: Unusual ways to change behavior.* San Francisco: Jossey-Bass.

(1985). *Conversations with Milton H. Erickson, M.D., Vol. 1: Changing individuals; Vol. 2: Changing couples; Vol. 3: Changing children and families.* New York: Triangle Press/W. W. Norton.

(1985). Remembering Erickson: A dialogue between Jay Haley and John Weakland. In J. K. Zeig (Ed.), *Ericksonian Psychotherapy, Vol. 1: Structures.* New York: Brunner-Mazel.

(1985). A review of ordeal therapy. In J. K. Zeig (Ed.), *Ericksonian Psychotherapy, Vol. 2: Clinical Applications.* New York: Brunner-Mazel.

(1986). *The power tactics of Jesus Christ* (2nd ed.). Rockville, MD: Triangle Press.

(1987). Problem-solving therapy (2nd ed.). San Francisco: Jossey-Bass.

(1987). Therapy—A new phenomenon. In J. K. Zeig (Ed.), *The evolution of psychotherapy.* New York: Brunner-Mazel.

(1988). Reflections on supervision. In H. A. Liddle et al. (Eds.), *Handbook of family therapy training and supervision.* New York: Guilford.

(1989). The effect of long-term outcome studies on the therapy of schizophrenia. *Journal of Marriage and Family Therapy, 15*(2), 127-132.

1990s

(1990). Why not long-term therapy? In J. K. Zeig (Ed.), *Brief therapy: Myths, methods, and metaphors.* New York: Brunner-Mazel.

(1991). *Conversations on therapy: Popular problems and uncommon solutions.* New York: W. W. Norton. With David R. Grove.

(1992). Compulsory therapy for both the client and the therapist. *Family Psychology and Counseling, 1*(2), 1-7.

(1992). Zen and the art of therapy. In J. K. Zeig (Ed.), *The evolution of psychotherapy.* New York: Brunner-Mazel.

(1993, fall). How to be a therapy supervisor without knowing how to change anyone. *Journal of Systemic Therapies, 12*(4), 41-52.

(1993). *Jay Haley on Milton Erickson.* New York: Brunner-Mazel.

(1993). A model therapy for psychotic young people. In *Leaving home: The therapy of disturbed young people* (2nd ed.). New York: Brunner-Mazel. With N. P. Schiff.

(1994). Erickson hypnotic demonstration: 1964. In S. R. Lankton & K. K. Erickson (Eds.), *Erickson Monographs Number 9: The essence of a single session success.* New York: Brunner-Mazel.

(1994). Typically Erickson. In J. K. Zeig (Ed.), *Ericksonian methods: The essence of the story.* New York: Brunner-Mazel.

(1995). John Weakland: A personal note. *Family Process, 35*(4), 369-371.

(1996). *Learning and teaching therapy.* New York: Guilford Publishers.

(1997). Changes in therapy. In J. Zeig (Ed.), *The evolution of psychotherapy.* New York: Brunner-Mazel.

(1997). *Leaving home: The therapy of disturbed young people* (2nd ed.). New York: Brunner-Mazel.

2000s

(2000). Computer monitor supervision: A clinical note. *American Journal of Family Therapy, 28,* 275-282. With C. R. Scherl.

(2001). The loyal opposition. In J. K. Zeig (Ed.), *Changing directives: The strategic therapy of Jay Haley.* Phoenix: Zeig, Tucker & Theisen.

(2003). *The art of strategic therapy.* New York: Brunner/Routledge. With M. Richeport-Haley.

(2003). What therapists have in common. In J. K. Zeig (Ed.), *The evolution of psychotherapy: A meeting of the minds.* Phoenix: The Milton H. Erickson Foundation Press.

(2006). *The Power Tactics of Jesus Christ and Other Essays.* Norwalk, CT: Crown House Publishing Ltd.

(2006). *Strategies of Psychotherapy.* Norwalk, CT: Crown House Publishing Ltd.

UNPUBLISHED MANUSCRIPTS AND PAPERS

(1956). *A hypothesis regarding the origin and nature of schizophrenia.*

(1957). *Explorer in hypnosis.*

(1965). *Communication in learning and psychotherapy.*

(1977). *Social control vs. therapy.*

(1982). *On the right to choose one's own grandchildren.*

(1993). *The dual hierarchy and power in marriage.*

(1993). *The dual hierarchy and the problems of children.*

(1993). *Sex and power in marriage.*

(1993). *Therapist abuse.*

(1994). *Alternate views of "schizophrenia" and their consequences to therapy.*

(1994). *A matter of character by the ghost of Gregory Bateson.* With M. Richeport-Haley.

(1996, June). *Brave men run in my family.* Paper presented at the meeting of the Men's Project. Washington, DC.

(1996). *The brief, brief therapy of Milton H. Erickson, MD.* Paper presented at the Brief Therapy Conference sponsored by the Milton H. Erickson Foundation, San Francisco, CA.

AUDIO PROGRAMS AND TELEVISION PLAYS

(1960s). An anxious husband and an erring wife. Unpublished one-hour television play.

(1960s). The red and the black. An unpublished live television play adapted from the novel by Stendahl.

(1960s). The small monster. In the series *Eleventh hour.* Unpublished one-hour television play.

(1962). The lady was a gentleman. In the series *Headshrinker.*

(1989). *The first therapy session.* San Francisco: Jossey-Bass Audio Programs.

(1991). *Milton H. Erickson, M.D., In His Own Voice. 1. Sex Therapy: The Female (2 hours); 2. Sex Therapy: The Male (2 hours); 3. Problem Drinker (1 hour); 4. Multiple Personality (1 hour).* New York: W. W. Norton. With M. Richeport-Haley.

(n.d.). *How to interview clients and identify problems successfully.* San Francisco: Jossey-Bass Audio Programs.

FOREIGN TRANSLATIONS

Chinese

(2004). *Problem-solving therapy.* Taipei, Taiwan: Wu-Nan Book, Inc.

Czech

(2003). *Neobvykla psychoterapie. Miltona H. Ericksona.* Praha: Triton.

Dutch

(1963). *Strategieen in de psychotherapie.* Amsterdam-Utrecht: Erven J. Bijleveld.

(1974). *De machtspolitiek van Jezus Christus.* Amsterdam: Den Haag.

(1975). *Buitengewone therapie de methoden van Milton H. Erickson.* Nederlandse De Toorts.

(1978). *Directieve gezins-therapie.* Nederlandse De Toorts.

Finnish

(1997). *Lyhytterapian lahteilla.* Milton H. Erikcsonin Terapeuttiset Menetelmat. Mieli-Kirjat.

French

(1979). *Nouvelles strategies en therapie familiak: La problem-solving en psychotherapie familiak.* Paris: Jean-Pierre Delarge.

(1984). *Un therapeute hors du commun, Milton H. Erickson, M.D.* Paris: Hommes de Groupes.

(1985). *Changer les couples. Conversations avec Milton H. Erickson.* Paris: E S F editeur.

(1991). *Leaving home. Quand le jeune adulte quitte sa famille.* Paris: E S F editeur.

(1991). *Tacticiens du pouvoir: Jesus-Christ k psychanalyste, le schizophrene et quelques autres.* Paris: E S F editeur.

(1992). *Strategies de la psychotherapie.* Toulouse: Editions Eres.

German

(1978). *Die Psychotherapie Milton H. Ericksons.* Munchen: Pfeiffer.

(1981). *Abbsungsprobleme Jugendlicher Familientherapie.* Munchen: Pfeiffer.

(1989). *Ordeal Therapie.* Hamburg: ISKO-Press.

(1990). *Die Jesus-Strategic Die Mucht der Ohnmachtigen.* Basel: Aus d. Amerikan iibers von Ulrike Franke-Weinheim.

(1996). *Typisch Erickson Muster Seiner Arbeit.* Paderborn: Junfermann Verlag.

(2001). *Learning and teaching therapy.* Baarn: H. Buitgevers.

Hebrew

(1982). *Problem-solving therapy. New strategies for effective family therapy.* Tel-Aviv: Publishing House Ltd.

Italian

(1974). *Tecniche di terapia della famigk.* With L. Hofhan. Roma: Astrolabio.

(1976). *Terapie non comuni. Techiche ipnotiche e terapia della famiglia.* Roma: Casa Editrice Astrolabio-Ubaldini Editore.

(1983). *Il distucco della famiglia.* Roma: Casa Editrice Astrolabio.

(1984). *Le strategie della psicoterapia.* Firenze: Sansoni Studio.

(1985). *La terapia del problem-solving.* Nuove Strategie per unu Terapia Familiare Efficace. Roma: NIS.

(1988). *Cambiare I bambini e le famiglie, Conversazioni com Milton H. Erickson Vol. III.* Roma: Casa Editrice Astrolabio.

(1995). *Dietro lo specchio. Problemi ingarbugliati e soluzioni originuli nella terapia della famiglia.* With David Grove. Roma: Astrolabio.

(1997). *Formazione e supervisione in psicoterapia.* Trento: Edizioni Erickson.

Japanese

(1985). Problem-solving therapy. Tokyo: Kawashima Shoten.
(1997). *Conversations with Milton H. Erickson, M.D. Vol. 1: Changing individuals.* Tokyo: Japan Uni Agency.
(2001). *Conversations with Milton H. Erickson, M.D. Vol. 2: Changing couples.* Tokyo: Japan Uni Agency.
(2001). *Conversations with Milton H. Erickson, M.D. Vol. 3: Changing children and families.* Tokyo: Japan Uni Agency.
(2001). *Uncommon therapy: The psychiatric techniques of Milton H. Erickson, M.D.* Tokyo: Japan Uni Agency.
(n.d.). *Strategies of psychotherapy.* Reirnei Shobo.

Polish

(1995). *Niezwytka terapia. Techniki terapeutycme Miltona H. Ericksona.* Gdanskie.

Portuguese

(1991). *Terapia nao-convencional tecnicas psiquiatricas de Milton H. Erickson, M.D.* Sao Paulo: Surnmus.
(1998). *Aprendendo e ensinando terapia.* Porto Alegre: Artmed.

Spanish

(1966). *Estrategias en psicoterapia.* Barcelona: Ediciones Toray, s.a.
(1972). *Tacticas de poder de Jesucristo, y otros ensayos.* Buenos Aires: Editorial Tiempo Contemporaneo.

(1974). *Tratamiento del la familia*. Barcelona: Graficas Saturno, Andres Doria.

(1976). *Tecnias de terapia familiar*. Buenos Aires: Amorrortu editores. With L. Hoffman.

(1980). *Terapia no convencional. Las tecnicas psiquiatricas de Milton H. Erickson, M.D.* Buenos Aires: Amorrortu editores.

(1980). *Terapia para resolver problemas*. Buenos Aires: Amorrortu editores.

(1984). *Terapia de ordalia. Camonis inusudles para modificar la conducra*. Buenos Aires: Amorrortu.

(1994). *Las tacticas de poder de Jesucristo y otros ensayos*. Barcelona: Paidos.

(1996). *Conversaciones sobre terapia. Soluciones no convencionales para los problems de siempre*. Buenos Aires: Amorrortu. With David Grove.

(1997). *Apender y ensenar terapia*. Buenos Aires: Amorrortu.

(2006). *El arte de la terapia estrategica*. Barcelona: Paidos. With Madeleine Richeport-Haley.

(n.d.). *Trustornos de la amancipacion juvenil y terapia familiar*. Buenos Aires: Amorrortu.

Swedish

(1975). *Psykoterapi-strategi och teknik*. Stockholm: Natur och Kultur.

(1976). *Strategisk psykoterapi. Milton H. Ericksons psykiatriska tekniker*. Stockholm: Natur och Kultur.

(1979). *Familjeterapi*. Stockholm: Natur och Kultur.

(1982). *Flytta hemifian familjeterapi med storda undomar*. Stockholm: Natur och Kultur.

Appendix C

Films by Jay Haley
and Madeleine Richeport-Haley

Many of these films are available through Triangle Press, P. O. Box 8094, La Jolla, CA 92038 or at www.Jay-Haley-on-therapy.com.

Coming Home from the Mental Hospital (early 1970s)

An eighteen-year-old girl is hospitalized with a diagnosis of schizophrenia. The video narrated by Jay Haley shows the stages of helping her recover to normal activities as well as Jay Haley's supervision.

Heroin My Baby (1970s, 50 minutes enacted)

Edited by Jay Haley and Sam Kirschner, PhD, this video depicts the strategic therapy of a young man at the stage of leaving home. The youth is a heroin addict. Excerpts from the therapy interviews describe the theory and practical steps in the therapy. Narration guides the viewer through the issues and the approach.

A Modern Little Hans (1971, 50 minutes). Philadelphia Child Guidance Clinic.

The case of a boy who was afraid of dogs. The therapist directed the boy to adopt a puppy who was afraid and help the puppy get

Directive Family Therapy
Published by The Haworth Press, Inc., 2007. All rights reserved.
doi:10.1300/5883_12

over its fears by playing with it, thereby helping the boy to get over his own fears.

Only on Sunday (1972, 50 minutes). Philadelphia Child Guidance Clinic.

A ten-year-old boy's problem of public masturbation is resolved by encouraging excessive repetition of the symptomatic behavior to make it an ordeal.

Jay Haley on Strategic Therapy (1978, 50 minutes)

Interviewed by Richard Rabkin, MD, in 1978, Jay Haley discussed how to plan a therapy strategy and how to give directives to bring about change. The techniques are those of brief therapy.

Remembering Milton H. Erickson (1980s, 60 minutes)

A conversation between Jay Haley and John Weakland about their life and times when they consulted with Erickson about his brief therapy and the nature of hypnosis.

Strategic-Structural Therapy: Is There A Difference? A Conversation with Jay Haley and Salvador Minuchin (1980s, 50 minutes)

This video features a conversation on the basic issues of therapy and clinical training.

Macumba Trance and Spirit Healing (1984, 43 minutes)

Filmed primarily in Rio de Janeiro, this film shows the art of trance healing and expresses an Ericksonian approach. The film appeared on PBS.

Milton H. Erickson: *Explorer in Hypnosis and Therapy* (1993, 56 minutes)

This film chronicles Erickson's life, overcoming handicaps, and the innovation of medical hypnosis and therapy. Narrated by Jay Haley, this documentary offers an intimate and far-reaching portrait of this remarkable individual's life and work during abundant interviews and therapeutic sessions.

How Did You Meet Him? (1994, 50 minutes)

A group of Erickson enthusiasts describe their first meeting with him.

Dance and Trance of Balinese Children (1995, 45 minutes)

Combining footage taken by Gregory Bateson and Margaret Mead fifty years ago with footage today, this video shows how trance is learned through the dance and is passed on from generation to generation.

Approaching a Crisis: *Threats of Violence, Divorce and Suicide* (1997, 50 minutes enacted)

A therapist is expecting a child problem and finds himself while treating a family in crisis. The husband's threats of suicide and violence are dealt with in a human way by the therapist, who must choose to behave according to professional procedures or become personally involved. Jay Haley emphasizes the decisions that must be made as each new situation arises in the therapy process.

The Guaranteed Cure: *A Case of Bulimia/Anorexia* (1997, 50 minutes enacted)

This video illustrates how to persuade a client with an eating disorder to follow a directive. The bulimia is treated in the context of a marital couple, not individually. The primary directive is a promise that the cure is guaranteed if they do what the therapist says. However, the therapist will not tell them what the cure is until they promise to follow the directive.

Jay Haley Seminar on Clinical Hypnosis (1997, 55 minutes enacted)

A seminar for a class in therapy differentiates personal, research, and clinical hypnosis when one is trying to change someone. The techniques of hypnosis are illustrated with Milton H. Erickson's 1958 and 1964 archival films.

Remembering Gregory Bateson (1997, 78 minutes)

This video records a conversation between Jay Haley and John Weakland about Bateson. They describe the birth of the double-bind project and the ideas they shared and developed with Bateson over a decade of research, which included the birth of family therapy.

Whither Family Therapy? A Jay Haley Version (1997, 50 minutes)

This film is about the history of family therapy from the past to current issues. It includes the ideas and participants in Gregory Bateson's project on the "double bind" and the development of systems theory, the contribution of Milton H. Erickson, and Zen, all combined into the directive therapy approach. Included is rare material from forty years of interviews, seminars, and actual cases.

Who is Paul Riley? A Conversation Between Jay Haley and Braulio Montalvo (1997)

This is a discussion on contemporary therapy and the training of family counselors in the 1970s, when the poor were trained to assist the poor in a program organized by Salvador Minuchin, MD.

Unbalancing a Couple (**1998, 30 minutes**)

A therapist who has been taught to be neutral with a couple and not side with either spouse learns how to really take sides. The emphasis is on the rules of communication that couples follow, which are difficult to change unless the therapist gets personally involved.

Compulsory Therapy: A Case of Violence (**1999, 35 minutes**)

A minority family in which two brothers, high school teenagers, were accused and sentenced to probation and therapy for beating up a kid for a racial slur. Haley's directives involve bringing the whole family together to assure this will not occur again. The family proves to be a responsible one with the cultural patterns highlighted in such a way that one sees the damage that could have been done had this case been mishandled.

Family Therapy at a Distance: A Case of Depression (**1999, 55 minutes**)

This case of a Middle Eastern medical student shows the therapist learning to deal with a depressed man using a directive approach. The primary directive was to get the man to write a letter to his father. This proved to be a difficult one for the supervisor in relation to the therapist and the therapist in relation to the family. It illustrates the parallel between therapy and supervision. Haley arranges a change for them both.

Jay Haley on Directive Family Therapy (**1999, 40 minutes**)

A general lecture to a training group on Jay Haley's approach to therapy. He provides the viewer with an understanding of his practical teaching premises and information on a variety of issues.

These include family therapy and hypnosis, evolution of live supervision and brief, problem-focused case examples taken from his pioneering work in directive family therapy.

A Positive Approach with a Psychotic Couple (1999, 45 minutes)

This young couple had been in therapy and in and out of hospitals for years. The husband was diagnosed as schizophrenic and the wife with schizophrenic disorder. Both were incurable and were on permanent disability. Haley takes the approach that grew out of the ideas of Harry Stack Sullivan and Don Jackson that the clients should be treated as if nothing were wrong except the social situation. He directs the therapist to treat the couple as a normal one, despite extreme behavior of suicide threats. The consultation presents a way to make a fresh start in a chronic case.

The Boy Who Can't Stop Fighting (2001, 45 minutes)

Part of the *Learning and Teaching with Jay Haley* series. A case study of a problem child improved by the paradoxical approach.

Brief Strategic Therapy with Couples (2001, 50 minutes)

Part of the *Learning and Teaching with Jay Haley* series. This training film illustrates therapy techniques to be used with married couples in distress. The therapy presented here focuses on the problem sequences and uses directives to change them, particularly with the use of paradox.

How Many Clients Are in One Body? (2001, 45 minutes)

Part of the *Learning and Teaching with Jay Haley* series. A trainee seeing her first case learns to make a diagnosis with a Brazilian woman whose pathology was expressed in cultural beliefs.

Family Therapy in Bali **(2004, 30 minutes)**

This video presents a series of cases seen by Balinese healers. It reveals and examines the similarities between Balinese healing methods and the hypnotic techniques of Milton Erickson and the strategic family therapy approach of Jay Haley.

Index

Directive Family Therapy
Published by The Haworth Press, Inc., 2007. All rights reserved.
doi:10.1300/5883_13